Special Educational Needs for Qualified and Trainee Teachers

This completely revised and updated edition, previously published as *Special Educational Needs for Newly Qualified Teachers and Teaching Assistants,* addresses the latest Teachers' Standards and their application in meeting the most recent developments and changes in the special educational needs and disability (SEND) system and the new draft 2014 *SEND Code of Practice.*

Essential reading and an invaluable guide for all qualified, newly qualified and trainee teachers, this highly practical text relates to those accessing SEND training via teaching school alliances, as well as higher education.

Full of tips and strategies on how to meet the needs of a diversity of children and young people with SEND in a range of educational settings, chapters cover:

- the latest Teachers' Standards aligned to the most recent SEND changes;
- the draft 2014 *SEND Code of Practice*, the Children and Families Act, and the Equality Act and its related Duties;
- teaching schools, specialist leaders of education in SEND, and new training models for building teacher capacity in SEND;
- how to meet the latest Ofsted inspection requirements for SEND;
- what works best in the effective teaching of pupils with SEND and those eligible for the pupil premium.

Featuring useful checklists, templates, photocopiable and downloadable resources to support professional development in SEND, this practical resource contains a wealth of valuable advice, in addition to signposting to further information.

This no-nonsense, down-to-earth and authoritative text will provide essential reading for all experienced, qualified, newly qualified and trainee teachers, as well as to those delivering SEND training in higher education, local authorities, and in teaching schools and their alliances.

Rita Cheminais is a freelance education consultant, author and national speaker.

Special Educational Needs for Qualified and Trainee Teachers

A practical guide to the new changes

Third edition

Rita Cheminais

Routledge
Taylor & Francis Group

LONDON AND NEW YORK

Third edition published 2015
by Routledge
2 Park Square, Milton Park, Abingdon, Oxon OX14 4RN

and by Routledge
711 Third Avenue, New York, NY 10017

Routledge is an imprint of the Taylor & Francis Group, an informa business

© 2015 Rita Cheminais

First edition published 2000 by David Fulton Publishers

British Library Cataloguing in Publication Data
A catalogue record for this book is available from the British Library

Library of Congress Cataloging in Publication Data
Cheminais, Rita.
  Special educational needs for qualified and trainee teachers :
  a practical guide to the new changes / Rita Cheminais. — Third edition.
    pages cm
  Includes bibliographical references and index.
  1. Special education—Great Britain. 2. Children with mental disabilities—
  Education—Great Britain. 3. First year teachers—Great Britain. 4. Teachers'
  assistants—Great Britain. I. Title.
  LC3986.G7C47 2015
  371.90941—dc23   2014025867

ISBN: 978-1-138-77560-2 (hbk)
ISBN: 978-1-138-77561-9 (pbk)
ISBN: 978-1-315-73583-2 (ebk)

Typeset in Bembo
by Keystroke, Station Road, Codsall, Wolverhampton

Printed and bound in the United States of America by
Edwards Brothers Malloy on sustainably sourced paper

Contents

Contents

Figures

Tables

Acknowledgements

I would like to thank the reviewers of this initial book proposal for their constructive comments, which helped to inform the new content for the revised third edition.

I would like to thank my commissioning editor Alison Foyle and Vicky Parting and Freya Davidson–Smith from Routledge Education for their patience, and for guiding and supporting me throughout the production of this book.

I wish to thank the Education Endowment Foundation (EEF) for granting permission to include the pupil premium approaches and their impact in Table 1.2, the National Association of Head Teachers (NAHT) for granting permission to make reference to their underpinning principles for assessment in schools in Table 4.1 and the DfE for granting permission to make reference to Charlie Taylor's behaviour checklist in Figure 5.3.

The publishers have made every effort to contact authors/copyright holders of works reprinted in *Special Educational Needs for Qualified and Trainee Teachers*, third edition. If we have been unable to trace any copyright holder then we welcome correspondence from those individuals/companies.

Abbreviations

ABA	Anti-Bullying Alliance
ABC	antecedents, behaviour, consequences
ADD	attention deficit disorder
ADHD	attention deficit hyperactivity disorder
AfL	assessment for learning
ASD	autistic spectrum disorder
BESD	behavioural, emotional and social difficulties
CaF	Contact a Family
CAMHS	Child and Adolescent Mental Health Service
CCG	clinical commissioning group
CEOP	Child Exploitation and Online Protection Centre
CFS	chronic fatigue syndrome
CPD	continuing professional development
CUREE	Centre for the Use of Research & Evidence in Education
DCSF	Department for Children, Schools and Families
DfE	Department for Education
DH	Department of Health
EAL	English as an additional language
EEF	Education Endowment Foundation
EHC	education, health and care
EHRC	Equality and Human Rights Commission
EYFS	Early Years Foundation Stage
FE	further education
FFT	Fischer Family Trust
FSM	free school meals
HI	hearing impairment
HRBQ	Health Related Behaviour Questionnaire
ICT	information and communication technology
IDP	Inclusion Development Programme
IEP	individual education plan
INSET	in-service education and training
ITT	initial teacher training
LA	local authority
LAC	looked after child/children

Abbreviations

LDA	Learning Difficulty Assessment
LSCB	Local Safeguarding Children's Board
ME	myalgic encephalitis
MLD	moderate learning difficulties
MSI	multi-sensory impairment
NAHT	National Association of Head Teachers
nasen	National Association for Special Educational Needs
NC	national curriculum
NCSL	National College for School Leadership
NCTL	National College for Teaching and Leadership
NEET	not in education, employment or training
NFER	National Foundation for Educational Research
NGA	National Governors' Association
NPQH	National Professional Qualification for Headship
NQT	newly qualified teacher
OCD	obsessive compulsive disorder
ODD	oppositional defiance disorder
Ofqual	Office for Qualifications and Examinations Regulation
Ofsted	Office for Standards in Education, Children's Services and Skills
PASS	Pupil Attitude to Self and School
PD	physical disability
PMLD	profound and multiple learning difficulties
PSED	Public Sector Equality Duty
PSHE	personal, social and health education
QTS	qualified teacher status
RAISE	Reporting and Analysis for Improvement through School
SEAL	social, emotional aspects of learning
SEN	special educational needs
SENCO	special educational needs coordinator
SEND	special educational needs and disabilities
SENDIST	Special Educational Needs and Disability Tribunal
SLCN	speech, language and communication needs
SLD	severe learning difficulties
SLE	specialist leader of education
SMSC	spiritual, moral, social and cultural
SpLD	specific learning difficulties
TA	teaching assistant
TAC	team around the child
TAF	team around the family
TEAM	together each achieves more
TIB	this is because
VAK	visual, auditory and kinaesthetic
VI	visual impairment
WALT	what are we learning to
WILF	what I'm looking for
YOT	Youth Offending Team

Introduction

The aim of this book

The overarching aim of this book is to help trainee, newly qualified and experienced class and subject teachers, working in a range of educational settings – from early years settings, to maintained primary and secondary schools, free schools and academies – to meet the government's latest special educational needs and disability (SEND) legal requirements, in order to ensure that they are alert to any emerging learning difficulties children with SEND may have, and in turn, be able to respond early to remove barriers to learning and participation.

In particular, the book aims to help all those working towards and with qualified teacher status (QTS) to:

- meet the latest Teachers' Standards, aligned to the most recent SEND reforms, as specified in the draft 2014 *SEND Code of Practice* (DfE/DH 2014g), the SEND Regulations 2014, Part 3 of the Children & Families Act 2014, and the Duties in the Equality Act 2010;

- meet the latest Office for Standards in Education, Children's Services and Skills (Ofsted) inspection requirements and expectations in SEND;

- ensure that pupils with SEND have access to high-quality teaching and learning that improves progress and outcomes;

- know what practice and provision works best for pupils with SEND, including those who are eligible for the pupil premium;

- access downloadable online resources that accompany this book, which can be tailored and customised to suit the context of the education setting;

- signpost to other practical continuing professional development resources to help to build capacity among teachers in the area of SEND.

Developments in SEND professional development to build staff capacity

As soon as the coalition government came into office in early May 2010, a raft of new SEND legislation brought about the biggest and most radical change in the SEND system in England since 1981, when statements of SEND were first introduced.

Alongside these new SEND reforms, a number of accompanying educational developments in relation to initial teacher training (ITT) and the continuing professional development (CPD) of teachers occurred, which saw a major shift away from local authority-centralised responsibility for school improvement and the delivery of CPD for teachers and support staff, to a school-based model for building capacity among school staff.

The list below outlines the government's main developments in building workforce capacity to meet the needs of pupils with SEND more effectively, which have taken place from 2010 onwards:

- They published the revised Teachers' Standards, which define the minimum level of practice expected of trainee, newly qualified and experienced teachers, along with the revised school teachers' performance appraisal regulations, both effective from 1 September 2012, which further strengthened the focus on support for children with additional needs, including those with SEND. For example, Teachers' Standard 5 requires teachers to have

  > a clear understanding of the needs of all pupils, including those with special educational needs; those of high ability; those with English as an additional language; those with disabilities; and be able to use and evaluate distinctive teaching approaches to engage and support them.
  >
  > (DfE 2013f: 12)

  The draft 2014 *SEND Code of Practice* also recommended:

  > The quality of teaching for pupils with SEN, and the progress made by pupils, should be a core part of the school's performance management arrangements and its approach to professional development for all teaching and support staff.
  >
  > (DfE 2014g: 6.4)

- They enabled the providers of ITT to secure a greater number of trainee teacher placements in special school settings.
- They included learning and best practice from the Achievement for All programme in the SEND training resources for ITT, as well as offering an optional module on Leading Inclusion: Achievement for All in the National Professional Qualification for Headship (NPQH).
- They developed SEND CPD materials to support the induction of newly qualified teachers (NQTs).
- They provided free advanced online multi-media interactive SEND training resources for class and subject teachers to access, which covered high-incidence and low-incidence types of SEND.
- They offered an annual national scholarship scheme to those qualified teachers wishing to deepen their knowledge and further develop their practice in supporting pupils with SEND by undertaking a specialist postgraduate qualification.
- They offered an annual national scholarship fund to the most able and talented support staff (i.e. teaching assistants (TAs)), to help them to gain a degree-level qualification to further improve their knowledge and expertise in SEND, with the potential to pursue a career in teaching.

- They continued to fund the mandatory national training of newly appointed SEN coordinators (SENCOs), the National Award in SEN Coordination, which gives new SENCOs the skills and knowledge to model effective SEND practice and to advise class and subject teachers in their own education setting on how best to meet the needs of SEND pupils in the mainstream.

- They introduced and developed a network of teaching schools, some of which share their expertise in SEND and behaviour management with other local schools, particularly those who require improvement in either of these aspects, in addition to providing high-quality training and CPD in SEND to trainee, newly qualified and experienced teachers. Teaching schools were also given the responsibility to broker support for other schools requiring improvement from local specialist leaders of education (SLEs). In their White Paper *The Importance of Teaching*, the Department for Education (DfE) commented: 'We know that teachers learn best from other professionals and that an "open classroom" culture is vital' (DfE 2010a: 2.4).

- They introduced SLEs, some of whom have expertise in SEND or behaviour management, to support teachers in other schools to improve their practice in the particular aspect. In their 2011 SEND Green Paper *Support and Aspiration: A New Approach to Special Educational Needs and Disability – A Consultation*, the DfE commented:

  > We will create a new designation of specialist leaders of education. These will be serving middle and senior school leaders who are outstanding at what they do and who are able to play a role beyond their own school, supporting others to improve, including those who work with children with SEN and disabilities.
  >
  > (DfE 2011b: 3.22)

- They increased the focus on SEND in Ofsted inspections, in order to keep under review the impact of the DfE's SEND reforms in improving the provision and outcomes for children and young people with SEND in early years settings, schools and academies.

The government considered that with all the above strategies in place, teachers would feel better equipped and more confident in identifying SEND and removing barriers to learning and participation experienced by pupils with SEND. In addition, the government envisaged that through school-based training and evidence-based CPD approaches, teachers would feel more able to identify effectively what pupils with SEND need in order to help them to learn better, and to plan support to assist those pupils to make good and outstanding progress.

In view of the DfE expecting every teacher to be responsible and accountable for the progress and development of pupils with SEND, even when they may be accessing additional support from TAs or specialist staff outside the mainstream classroom, this book goes some way to enable busy trainee and qualified teachers to rise to the government's challenge.

How the book is designed to be used

The book can be worked through systematically in chapter order, or it can be dipped into, focusing on particular areas of interest. Either way, this practical book provides an invaluable resource for trainee, newly qualified and experienced teachers that can be used to:

- act as a quick point of reference for busy practitioners working in a range of educational settings, from early years to post-16, as well as for those leading SEND training via teaching school alliances, and in higher education institutions;

- inform the development of a more consistent approach to meeting the needs of pupils with SEND that responds appropriately to the government's latest SEND reforms;

- promote further professional dialogue and reflection among teachers, at all stages in their career, on what works best in relation to teaching pupils with SEND;

- complement the SEND training modules used on ITT, NQT and NPQH programmes;

- enable pages of the book to be photocopied, and resources to be downloaded for developmental purposes, within the purchasing organisation or service.

CHAPTER 1

Working within the law and frameworks for SEND

This chapter covers:

- Demystifying the terminology
- Legislation and developments in SEND from 2010 to 2014
- The Children and Families Act 2014, Part 3
- The draft 2014 *SEND Code of Practice (0 to 25)*
- The Equality Act 2010 and its related Duties
- Ofsted inspections and SEND
- Teachers' professional development for SEND
- The concept, use and impact of the pupil premium

Demystifying the terminology

The definition of SEND

A child or young person has SEND if he or she has a learning difficulty or disability that calls for special educational provision to be made for him or her. A child of compulsory school age or a young person has a learning difficulty or disability if he or she:

> **(a)** has a significantly greater difficulty in learning than the majority of others of the same age; or
>
> **(b)** has a disability which prevents or hinders him or her from making use of educational facilities of a kind generally provided for others of the same age in mainstream schools or mainstream post-16 institutions.
>
> (DfE 2014g: 4 xi–xii)

Special educational provision is educational or training provision that is additional to or different from that made generally for others of the same age. This means provision that goes beyond the differentiated approaches and learning arrangements normally provided as part of high-quality, personalised teaching. It may take the form of additional support from within the setting or require the involvement of specialist staff or support services.

The definition of disability

A child has a disability if they have a physical or mental impairment, and the impairment has a substantial and long-term adverse effect on their ability to carry out normal day-to-day activities (i.e. lasts for twelve months or more). The disability prevents or hinders the child or young person from making use of educational facilities of a kind generally provided for others of the same age.

Examples of disabilities

Disability covers a wide range of impairments. Teachers need to be aware of the diversity of pupils, who, under the Equality Act 2010, are considered to have a disability. These include:

- sensory impairments (e.g. visual impairment (VI), hearing impairment (HI) and multi-sensory impairment (MSI));
- physical impairments or illnesses that affect mobility, dexterity or control of movement (e.g. arthritis, multiple sclerosis, stroke);
- developmental conditions (e.g. dyslexia, dyspraxia, autistic spectrum);
- progressive diseases (e.g. motor neurone disease, muscular dystrophy, dementia, lupus);
- illnesses with impairments with fluctuating or recurring effects (e.g. myalgic encephalitis (ME), chronic fatigue syndrome (CFS), epilepsy, diabetes);
- mental health conditions and mental illnesses (e.g. depression, eating disorders, obsessive compulsive disorder (OCD), schizophrenia, bipolar affective disorders, self-harm);
- HIV infection;
- cancer;
- facial disfigurements.

Legislation and developments in SEND from 2010 to 2014

Since the coalition government came into power in May 2010, the review of the existing 2001 SEND system and its accompanying legislation has moved at a considerable pace. The Children and Families Act 2014, Part 3, with its SEND Regulations, and the draft 2014 *SEND Code of Practice (0 to 25)* have brought about the most radical reforms to SEND since the introduction of the statement of SEN in 1981. Figure 1.1 provides an overview of the developments in SEND from 2010 to 2014.

The Children and Families Act 2014, Part 3

The Children and Families Bill gained Royal Assent on 13 March 2014 to become the Children and Families Act, effective from 1 September 2014. Part 3 of the Act relates to SEND.

In summary, the Children and Families Act 2014, Part 3 has brought about the following changes:

Equality Act 2010

The Act replaced previous Acts and regulations related to race, disability and gender equality and discrimination to provide one comprehensive law covering all types of discrimination. The Duties in Chapter 1 of Part 6 of the Act apply to schools and other education settings.

The Act places two important duties on schools:

1. **General Public Sector Equality Duty (PSED)** – eliminate unlawful discrimination, harassment and victimisation; advance equality of opportunity; foster good relations.
2. **Specific Duties** – publish information to show compliance with the General Duty; prepare and publish specific and measurable equality objectives every four years.

Progression 2010–11: Advice on Improving Data to Raise Attainment and Maximise the Progress of Learners with Special Educational Needs (DfE)

The DfE updated the previous 2009 version of this guidance to include revised data sets.

Special Educational Needs and Disability Review: A Statement Is Not Enough (Ofsted)

This focused on three aspects: assessment and identification; access to and quality of provision; evaluation and accountability. The review evaluated how well the SEND legislative framework was serving children and young people with SEND, from early years up to the age of 19. The findings from this review helped to inform the coalition government's subsequent 2014 SEND reforms.

Support and Aspiration: A New Approach to Special Educational Needs and Disability (DfE)

This SEND Green Paper was published in March 2011. It set out the coalition government's vision for a new SEND system and recommended the following improvements:

– identification of SEND early with support put in place quickly;
– staff to know and understand SEND and have the skills to meet the needs of pupils with SEND;
– raise aspirations through an increased focus on outcomes for pupils with SEND;
– parents better informed about what local schools, colleges, the LA and local services provide for pupils with SEND;
– parents to have more of a say over the services being used;
– Education, Health and Care (EHC) plan and an integrated assessment process for those children and young people aged 0–25 with more complex needs.

SEND pathfinders (DfE, October 2011)

The DfE established 20 SEND pathfinder trials, covering 31 LAs, to test the proposals in the 2011 SEND Green Paper. Six aspects explored further by the SEND pathfinders included: introduction of a new single 0–25 coordinated assessment process and EHC planning; the local offer; personal budgets; joint commissioning; engagement and participation of pupils with SEND and their parents and carers; preparing for adulthood. The lessons learned from the SEND pathfinders helped to inform and support the implementation of the SEND reforms.

Support and Aspiration: A New Approach to Special Educational Needs and Disability – Progress and Next Steps (DfE, May 2012)

The coalition government's plan for action set out the next stages in developing new SEND legislation. In brief:

– streamlined, quicker single assessment process, involving pupils with SEND and their families more;
– EHC plan to replace SEND statements, focused on outcomes, bringing services together;
– personal budgets for those with an EHC plan;
– LAs and health services joint planning and commissioning, to meet the needs of pupils with SEND and their families;
– LAs to publish their local offer;
– mediation to resolve disputes and a tribunal system introduced, giving pupils with SEND the right to appeal if they are unhappy with their support and provision.

Draft Legislation on the Reform of Provision for Children and Young People with Special Educational Needs (DfE, September 2012)

This outlined the draft legislation required to put the DfE's SEND proposals into practice.

The document was in two parts:

Part 1 – clarified the legislation and duties for identifying SEND, assessing needs and making SEND provision.

Part 2 – explanatory notes prepared by the DfE to be read in conjunction with the draft legislation.

continued

The Framework for School Inspection **(Ofsted, September 2012)**
The revised inspection schedule focused on four key areas:

1. the quality of leadership and management;
2. the behaviour and safety of pupils;
3. the quality of teaching;
4. the achievement of pupils.

Inspections also consider:

– the extent to which the education provided by the school meets the needs of pupils who have a disability for the purposes of the Equality Act 2010, and who have SEND;
– spiritual, moral, social and cultural (SMSC) development of pupils at the school.

A revised ***School Inspection Handbook*** was published by Ofsted to support the inspection framework, along with ***Subsidiary Guidance*** for supporting inspectors undertaking Section 5 school inspections. This included guidance on the achievement of pupils with SEND; the behaviour of pupils with SEND; special schools, and mainstream schools with resourced SEND provision.

The Framework for School Inspection, the *School Inspection Handbook* and *Subsidiary Guidance* were further revised in January 2014 and again in July 2014.

Working Together to Safeguard Children: A Guide to Inter-Agency Working to Safeguard and Promote the Welfare of Children **(DfE, March 2013)**
Statutory guidance came into force in April 2013, replacing earlier guidance. It clarified responsibilities of professionals safeguarding children and young people, shifting the focus away from processes onto needs; it indicated the key factors making effective safeguarding systems; it emphasised two essential principles that underpin effective safeguarding arrangements:

1. Safeguarding is everyone's business.
2. A child-centred approach ensures a clear understanding of the needs and views of children and young people.

Five chapters in the revised guidance cover:

1. Accessing need and providing help;
2. Organisational responsibilities;
3. Local Safeguarding Children's Boards (LSCBs);
4. Learning and improvement framework;
5. Child death reviews.

The revised guidance improves timely information sharing and expert judgements among professionals to be used in order to safeguard children and young people promptly.

The Children and Families Bill 2013
This extended the SEND system to cater for those aged 0–25, taking forward the coalition government's SEND reform programme. It included measures to:

– give those in further education (FE) and training aged 16–25 the same rights as those in school;
– encourage LAs and health services to jointly commission education, health and social care services;
– encourage LAs to publish in one place a clear local offer of services for SEND;
– promote greater cooperation between LAs and other partners;
– encourage LAs to consult pupils with SEND and their parents in reviewing SEND and social care provision;
– introduce a more streamlined, integrated assessment process for those with more severe and complex needs;
– replace SEN statements and Learning Difficulty Assessments (LDAs) with an EHC plan, focused on outcomes and preparation for adulthood;
– encourage parents and pupils with SEND to go for mediation to resolve disagreements about provision, before going for a SEND Tribunal
– offer those with an EHC plan a personal budget.

The Bill came into force on 1 September 2014 as the Children and Families Act.

Indicative Draft: The (0–25) Special Educational Needs Code of Practice **(DfE, March 2013)**
This document helped parliament consider the SEND clauses in Part 3 of the Children and Families Bill, along with the related draft indicative regulations. The draft took account of feedback from consultation on the proposed SEND reforms. The indicative draft document supported the passage of the Children and Families Bill through the House of Lords during the summer of 2013.

It comprised of seven chapters, focused on:

1. Introduction to the new SEND system and SEND Code of Practice
2. Family-centred system
3. EHC integration, joint commissioning and cooperation
4. Local offer
5. Policy into practice for education settings
6. Assessments and EHC plans
7. Resolving disputes.

Draft Special Educational Needs (SEN) Code of Practice: for 0 to 25 Years – Statutory Guidance for Organisations Who Work with and Support Children and Young People with SEN (DfE/DH, October 2013)
This draft document for consultation provided practical advice on how to carry out statutory duties to identify, assess and make provision for children and young people with SEN. The guidance in the *SEN Code of Practice* refers to Part 3 of the Children and Families Bill and associated regulations.

There were nine chapters in the draft *SEN Code of Practice*, which covered:

1. Introduction
2. Summary
3. Family-centred system
4. Working together across education, health and care
5. Local offer
6. Improving outcomes for all
7. Assessments and EHC plans
8. Children and young people in specific circumstances
9. Resolving disputes.

Following consultation and amendments, the *SEN Code of Practice (0 to 25)* came into force on 1 September 2014, along with the provisions in the Children and Families Bill and its associated regulations.

Draft Regulations (October 2013) associated with the Children and Families Bill

– SEN (Local Offer) Regulations, Clause 30
– Remaining in special school or post-16 institution without an EHC plan Regulations, Clause 34
– Education (SEN) (Assessment & Plan) Regulations, Clauses 37, 44 and 45
– The Approval of Independent Educational Institutions & Special Post-16 Institutions Regulations, Clause 41
– The SEN (Personal Budgets & Direct Payments) Regulations, Clause 49
– The SEN (Appeal) Regulations, Clause 51
– The SEN (Mediation) Regulations, Clause 52
– The SEN (Children's Rights to Appeal Pilot Scheme) Order, Clause 54
– The SEN (SEN Co-ordinators) Regulations, Clause 63 (updating previous 2008 SENCO Regulations and clarifying the extended SENCO role, to meet the new 2014 SEN legislative framework)
– The SEN (Information) Regulations, Clause 65
– Policy statement on regulations (Transitional arrangements), Clause 109.

Several of these Regulations became the **Special Educational Needs and Disability Regulations 2014**.

Supporting Pupils at School with Medical Conditions: Statutory Guidance for Governing Bodies of Maintained Schools and Proprietors of Academies in England (DfE, February 2014)
This draft guidance covered: school medical policies; content of pupil healthcare plans; roles and responsibilities of the governing body, head, staff, the LA and external practitioners (e.g. school nurse); training for school staff supporting pupils with medical needs and giving medication; managing medicines on school premises; record keeping; safe storage of medication; arrangements for pupils with medical needs going on day trips, residential visits, and participating in sporting activities; home-to-school transport arrangements.

Children and Families Act 2014, Part 3 – Children and Young People in England with Special Educational Needs or Disabilities
This Act received Royal Assent on 13 March 2014, following several amendments being made to Part 3 of the Bill by the government. These amendments related to the inclusion of disabled children and young people within the scope of the legislation, which previously only covered children and young people with SEND in Part 3. The amendments have resulted in disabled children and young people being included in a number of clauses relating to the local offer, and in local joint commissioning arrangements. The amended clauses are 21, 22, 23, 24, 25, 26, 27, 30, 32, 34, 68 and 73.

continued

***Special Educational Needs and Disability: Research Priorities and Questions* (DfE, March 2014)**
This paper outlines the SEND priorities the DfE wishes to research in further depth. These include:

– how to measure the performance of the SEND system;
– the methods used by education settings to identify pupils with SEND;
– the teaching and learning approaches that have the greatest impact on the attainment of different groups of pupils with SEND;
– how England's approach to SEND compares to that of other countries;
– the impact that different types of support have on SEND pupil outcomes;
– which are the most effective approaches to assess the achievement of pupils with SEND;
– how integrated working across services is impacting on pupils with SEND;
– how changes in teacher education are impacting on teacher competence and confidence in identifying and supporting pupils with SEND.

***The SEN and Disability Pathfinder Programme Evaluation: Progress and Indicative Costs of the Reforms – Research Report* (DfE, March 2014)**

This report feeds back on the progress made by 31 SEND pathfinder LA areas in preparing for and meeting the government's forthcoming SEND reforms.

Overall, the majority of LA SEND pathfinders are addressing change management, but are less advanced in setting up the infrastructure for meeting the government's SEND reforms. For example, few had implemented a system for managing personal budgets for SEND; several LA pathfinders were still communicating and implementing their safeguarding information with families and providers; the development of the local offer remained less well developed in several LA pathfinder areas; most SEND pathfinder LAs were engaging with parents and carers and the voluntary/community sectors to inform service provision, but just under half of the SEND pathfinder LAs were consulting with children and young people sufficiently to inform the local offer and service provision.

***Draft Special Educational Needs and Disability Code of Practice: 0 to 25 Years – Statutory Guidance for Organisations Who Work with and Support Children and Young People with Special Educational Needs and Disabilities* (DfE/DH, April 2014)**
This third draft version added the word 'disability' to the title of the document and made several other improvements, following consultation:

– Schools' statutory and non-statutory duties are clearer.
– Joint commissioning is explained more clearly.
– Clearer information is provided on how LAs will support SEND pupils aged post-16 and over 18, including transition to adulthood.
– School accountability for pupils on SEN Support without an EHC plan has been strengthened.
– LAs are to be more accountable for engaging service users in informing their local offer.
– More information has been given on the roles and responsibilities of different service providers.
– More detailed information is provided about where parents and carers can complain and seek redress if they are unhappy with provision.

This third draft version of the *SEND Code of Practice* is better structured to make it easier to navigate. New chapters have been added to separate out information for early years, schools and post-16 practitioners and on preparation for adulthood. Schools are advised to use this version as a planning tool, until the final *SEND Code of Practice* is published in summer 2014.

***Implementing a New 0 to 25 Special Needs System: LAs and Partners – Further Government Advice for Local Authorities and Health Partners* (DfE, April 2014)**
This information pack provides further guidance for LAs and their health partners (e.g. clinical commissioning groups (CCGs), Health & Well-Being Boards) on implementing the SEND reforms. It gives:

– a useful timeline for implementing the new SEND system;
– further guidance on implementing the LA local offer;
– further information about EHC plans;
– further information about personal budgets;
– a clearer outline of the support available to LAs to help them to implement the SEND reforms;
– further information about how to involve children, young people and their parents and carers more proactively in decisions about provision;
– further explanation on the role of the health service in implementing the new SEND system.

***Consultation on Draft Guidance for Supporting Pupils at School with Medical Conditions: Summary of Responses* (DfE, April 2014)**
This document reports back on the outcome from consultation on the DfE draft statutory guidance, published in February 2014. Overall, feedback was positive; however, the following issues were raised:

– greater clarity needed about the roles and responsibilities of local health services;
– greater clarity needed about the provision of staff training to support pupils with medical conditions in school;
– concerns about the role and capacity of the school nurse and other healthcare professionals (e.g. specialist nurses and children's community nurses).

***Keeping Children Safe in Education: Information for All School and College Staff* (DfE, April 2014)**
This eight-page document provides staff with a summary of the key statutory guidance featured in the full DfE publication, as well as signposting them to other sources of useful information. It is to be read alongside the DfE publication *Working Together to Safeguard Children*, which was issued in 2013.

***Keeping Children Safe in Education: Statutory Guidance for Schools and Colleges* (DfE, April 2014)**
The legal duties in this document further safeguard and promote the welfare of children. This guidance replaces *Safeguarding Children and Safer Recruitment in Education* (2006).

The 2014 statutory guidance is to be read alongside *Working Together to Safeguard Children* (2013) and is comprised of four parts:

Part 1 – Safeguarding information: types of abuse and neglect, specific safeguarding issues;
Part 2 – The management of safeguarding;
Part 3 – Safer recruitment;
Part 4 – Allegations of abuse made against teachers and other staff.

Care Act 2014
This Act is important because it has implications for young people moving from children's to adult health and social care services. The Act addresses the following:

– improving joint working between health and social care to provide improved integrated care;
– providing personal budgets for health and social care to offer greater choice of services;
– removing barriers in accessing integrated care;
– ensuring a named professional to oversee and coordinate integrated care provision for those with a Care Plan;
– providing better information for health and social care staff on clients' health and care needs and treatment, via an electronic database;
– improving support for those moving from one service to another (e.g. smoother transfer for young people moving from children's services to adult services, or from hospital to home);
– enabling adult social care services to assess young people under the age of 18.

The Care Act 2014 is referred to in the *SEND Code of Practice (0 to 25)*.

Figure 1.1 Developments in SEND 2010–14

- education, health and social care services working together more closely;

- children and young people with SEND and their families having a clearer understanding about the support and provision they can get, through the local authority (LA)'s 'local offer';

- different organisations working together to help children and young people with SEND, which includes those from the voluntary, community sector;

- children and young people with SEND, and their parents and carers, having more of a say about the support and provision they receive, by informing the LA's local offer;

- one integrated coordinated assessment, which looks holistically at the needs of the child or young person with SEND to provide the support and services required from education, health and social care services;

- one single education, health and care (EHC) plan, which is focused on outcomes and records the education, health and social care provision required, from birth to the age of 25, if necessary – this replaces the statement of SEN and the Learning Difficulty Assessment (LDA);

- personal budgets for young people with SEND and their parents and carers, which enable them to choose some or all of the provision required, if they so wish;

- mediation and appeal through the SEND Tier 1 Tribunal offered to parents and carers, young people and children with SEND, in order to sort out any disputes or differences of opinion about provision.

The draft 2014 *SEND Code of Practice (0 to 25)*

The draft 2014 *SEND Code of Practice (0 to 25)* replaces previous statutory guidance in the 2001 *SEN Code of Practice*. The 2014 *SEND Code of Practice (0 to 25)* became effective on 1 September 2014. It provides practical advice on how to carry out the statutory duties in relation to identifying, assessing and making provision for children and young people with SEND from birth to the age of 25.

The key principles underpinning the 2014 *SEND Code of Practice* are as follows:

- the views, wishes and feelings of children and young people with SEND, and of their parents and carers, to be taken into account;

- children, young people and their parents and carers to be involved in decision making about their own provision;

- children and young people's SEND to be identified, and the appropriate support and additional interventions to be put in place promptly;

- closer collaboration between education, health and social care services to provide support and high-quality provision for children and young people with SEND;

- greater choice and control for young people and their parents and carers over their support, through access to a personal budget for SEND;

- helping children and young people with SEND to achieve the best possible educational and well-being outcomes in preparation for adulthood, including independent living and employment.

The draft 2014 *SEND Code of Practice* expectations of teachers

The draft 2014 *SEND Code of Practice* states that teachers are responsible and accountable for the progress and development of the pupils in their class, even where pupils access support from TAs or specialist staff. In practice, this means every teacher:

- understanding the strategies to identify and support pupils with SEND;

- knowing about high-incidence SEND most frequently encountered in mainstream classrooms;

- identifying and reducing barriers to learning and participation;

- providing high-quality differentiated and personalised teaching;

- differentiating the curriculum to match the reading age and ability of pupils with SEND;

- making reasonable adjustments to ensure maximum access to the curriculum, to the learning environment and to information;

- deploying TAs and other supporting adults effectively;

- engaging pupils with SEND in assessing and reviewing their own learning and progress;

- tracking and monitoring the progress of pupils with SEND at least once every term, and adjusting teaching and learning support accordingly;
- planning and reviewing support and the progress made by pupils with SEND;
- listening to and understanding the concerns of parents and carers about their children's needs;
- involving parents and carers of pupils with SEND in the setting of academic and developmental targets, and the review of their children's outcomes.

What is new and different in the draft 2014 *SEND Code of Practice*

The main changes and differences from the previous 2001 *SEN Code of Practice* include:

- a wider age range covered (i.e. from birth to the age of 25);
- a clearer focus on the views of children and young people with SEND, and on their role in decision making about their additional provision;
- an increased emphasis on the joint planning and joint commissioning of services, to ensure closer cooperation between education, health and social care services;
- an improved coordinated single assessment process, and a new 0 to 25 Education, Health and Care (EHC) plan, for those with more complex needs, who previously had a statement of SEN and an LDA;
- new guidance on the support children and young people with SEND should receive in education and training settings;
- a greater focus on support that enables those with SEND to succeed in their education and make a successful transition to adulthood;
- a change in terminology from behavioural, emotional and social difficulties (BESD) to social, emotional and mental health;
- Action and Action Plus replaced by a single school-based category known as SEN Support, as part of the graduated approach to meeting needs;
- individual education plans (IEPs) replaced by a personalised planning approach, focused on outcomes;
- greater emphasis and expectation placed on class and subject teachers, taking ownership for the planning and reviewing of pupils' SEN support.

Table 1.1 provides a useful summary for teachers and trainee teachers on the 'graduated approach' for pupils on SEN Support, or with an EHC plan.

Table 1.1

Draft 2014 *SEND Code of Practice* graduated approach to SEND

	SEN Support	EHC plan
Which children and young people	Single category of SEND, school-based, replacing Action and Action Plus, for those whose needs can be met in the mainstream.	Education, Health and Care (EHC) plan for all those aged 0–25 who previously had a SEN statement or an LDA.
Triggers for intervention	Where a pupil falls behind their peers, or continues to make less than expected progress, given their age and starting point, and despite high-quality personalised teaching targeted at their area of weakness, and differentiated approaches being used.	Needs more complex and severe, where a pupil, despite the additional and different SEN Support being put in place in the education setting, continues to make little or no progress, and the SEND provision is no longer able to meet the pupil's needs.
Whose responsibility	The class or subject teacher with the SENCO both undertaking further assessment to identify whether the pupil has a significant learning difficulty. The parents or carers of the child are informed and consulted on SEN Support required. The class or subject teacher takes lead responsibility for planning and reviewing the pupil's SEN Support.	The LA conducts an integrated statutory EHC needs assessment, and prepares and issues an EHC plan (20-week timescale), when there is robust evidence from the education setting, multi-agency professionals, the parents or carers and the SEND pupil that such a plan is required. Where the LA does not issue an EHC plan, it gives reasons why to relevant parties (16-week timescale), and the pupil remains on SEN Support.
Nature of additional or different provision	Graduated approach – Assess, Plan, Do and Review: – personalised plan with stretching relevant academic/developmental targets; expected outcomes specified, and nature of provision; – evidence-based interventions; – additional support from within the school; – adaptations made to the support provided; – involvement of specialist staff or support service as appropriate; – termly review of pupil progress towards meeting targets set and achieving expected outcomes, involving parents or carers and the pupil with SEND, where appropriate.	Parents or carers and the pupil can request that the LA prepare a personal budget to deliver all or some of the provision, set out in the EHC plan. This provision is likely to cater for the holistic needs of the pupil, and can include: – weekend or holiday respite care, or short break; – personal assistant support during school holidays; – participation in sports activities or day trips with additional transport needs; – specialist equipment or learning aids (e.g. electronic communication tools, supportive software); – social worker support; – extra therapy services; – home modifications (e.g. ramp for wheelchair access); – transport to attend special school play scheme or to undertake work placement. The EHC plan is reviewed annually and any changes to provision made.

© 2015, *Special Educational Needs for Qualified and Trainee Teachers*, Rita Cheminais, Routledge.

The Equality Act 2010 and its related Duties

The Equality Act 2010 replaced and unified all existing equality legislation (e.g. the Race Relations Act, the Disability Discrimination Act and the Sex Discrimination Act). The Equality Act came into force in education settings in October 2010. Chapter 1, Part 6 of the Equality Act sets out the duties that apply to early years providers, schools, academies, post–16 institutions and local authorities.

Duties for education settings

Education settings must not discriminate against a child or young person or a prospective child or young person because of their disability, race, sex, gender reassignment, religion or belief, or sexual orientation or because they are pregnant. In addition, an education setting must not discriminate against a child or young person in relation to the following activities:

- admission to the education setting;
- the provision of education;
- access to any benefit, facility or service;
- exclusion from the education setting;
- subjection to any other detriment.

The Equality Act 2010 includes two Duties:

1 **General Public Sector Equality Duty (PSED)** – this requires education settings to have 'due regard' to the need to:
  - eliminate unlawful discrimination, harassment and victimisation;
  - advance equality of opportunity;
  - foster good relations.

2 **Specific Duties** – these aim to help education settings to meet the PSED. They are:
  - to publish information to show how they are complying with the PSED (the information must be updated annually); and
  - to prepare and publish at least one specific and measurable equality objective, at least every four years.

Making reasonable adjustments for pupils with SEND

The Equality Act 2010 and its related Duties links closely with health and safety legislation that requires the governing body and the headteacher to consider whether they have taken 'reasonable steps' by amending their health and safety policies, procedures and practices to ensure that pupils with SEND are not placed at a substantial disadvantage compared with their peers.

Reasonable adjustments are to be made in relation to:

- changing provisions, criteria or practices;
- providing auxiliary aids and services.

Schools are expected to provide an auxiliary aid or service for a disabled pupil when it would be reasonable to do so, and if such an aid would alleviate any substantial disadvantage.

The duty to make reasonable adjustments is also anticipatory (i.e. adjustments must be planned and put in place in advance to prevent any disadvantage occurring prior to a disabled child or young person's admittance to the education setting).

The draft 2014 *SEND Code of Practice* states:

> Schools ... must publish accessibility plans (and local authorities, accessibility strategies) setting out how they plan to increase access for disabled pupils to the curriculum, the physical environment and to information.
>
> (DfE 2014g: 6 xviii)

It is therefore every teacher's responsibility to ensure that pupils with a disability who they teach have access to the curriculum and extra-curricular activities; access to information in different formats (e.g. large print, symbols, subtitles on video clips, signing); and safe access to the learning environment and learning resources. The following two examples show how reasonable adjustments can be made.

Example 1

A pupil with cerebral palsy who is a wheelchair user goes on a school trip with his class to an outdoor education centre. The class are to go on a twelve-mile hike over difficult terrain. The wheelchair user is unable to do the hike for health and safety reasons. Therefore, the class teacher has planned an alternative activity, with additional support from a TA. A reasonable adjustment has been made to ensure that the pupil is included with his peers in an outdoor education experience/learning opportunity.

Example 2

A five-year-old child with a medical condition is incontinent and requires nappies to be changed throughout the day at school. The school installs changing facilities in the disabled toilet. It has health and safety procedures in place for dealing with any incontinence issues. A TA has been assigned specifically to meet the child's personal needs. The TA has been trained and has received advice and guidance from an external health professional about the management of the child's personal needs.

Effective classroom practice and access arrangements for disabled pupils

In relation to class and subject teachers' classroom practice in ensuring pupils with a disability and/or a medical need have good access to learning and participation, they must ensure that they:

- give additional time, where appropriate, to enable disabled pupils to complete tasks and activities;

- modify and personalise teaching and learning to meet disabled pupils' needs;

- take account of disabled pupils' pace of learning and the specialist aids and equipment they use;

- take account of the effort and concentration disabled pupils need when undertaking oral work, or when using visual aids;

- ensure that work is adapted, or offer alternative activities in those subjects, where pupils are expected to manipulate tools or equipment, or to use certain types of materials;

- allow opportunities for disabled pupils to take part in educational visits and out-of-school-hours extra-curricular and extended school activities;

- include approaches that allow pupils with HIs to learn about sound in Science and Music, and pupils with VIs to learn about light in Science, and to use visual resources and images both in Art and Design and in Design Technology;

- use assessment for learning (AfL) techniques appropriate to the individual needs and abilities of children or young people with disabilities and/or medical needs.

Figure 1.2 provides a useful checklist for teachers and trainee teachers to use as a point of reference, in order to ensure that disabled children and young people have physical access and curriculum access as well as access to information in alternative formats.

The following two cameos of good practice show how digital technology can enable pupils with more complex physical or medical needs to have a voice, in relation to their own provision and the support they need to access learning.

Multi-media advocacy

The young person with intellectual and communication difficulties can use an 'Easy Build Wiki Website' tool. It is password-protected for security, and the young person can log into Wiki with Makaton symbols, if typing is problematic.

Wiki uses a multi-media approach, using words, pictures, video clips and sound as ways of conveying the young person's preferences and viewpoints.

The aim of using Wiki is to build, compile and develop a personal multi-media-centred portfolio for the young person to use.

The opening page of the Wiki resembles a visual mind map, which has a number of sections that are important to the young person – for example, family; communication; mobility and care; school; social; having fun. Clicking on any of these sections opens another Wiki webpage for viewing or adding information to.

Parents and carers can upload and store photographs, videos and documents on Wiki. They can control who has access to this information.

Wiki can enable the young person to produce (with support) a training video for any new staff who work with them to view, giving guidance on (for instance) how to correctly fit splints.

Wiki can also enable greater consistency in practice to be maintained between home and school, in relation to the young person's development and learning.

There are short and longer versions of this model of good practice to view at www.youtube.com/watch?v=76q1U31ihw0 and bit.ly/sc214-53 respectively.

Curriculum access	YES	NO
Training accessed has helped you to meet the needs of pupils with disability	❏	❏
The curriculum you deliver in school promotes the access of pupils with disabilities	❏	❏
The extra-curricular activities you plan enable pupils with a disability to participate	❏	❏
Disabled pupils are able to work independently, in a pair, as a group and as a whole class	❏	❏
Additional time is given to those pupils with a disability or a medical need for task completion	❏	❏
The curriculum subject(s) you deliver acknowledge(s) diversity and difference positively	❏	❏
You have high expectations of pupils with a disability or medical need	❏	❏
You recognise and allow for the mental effort expended by some pupils with a disability	❏	❏

Physical access to the learning environment and resources	YES	NO
Pupils with a disability sit near the front of the class	❏	❏
Wheelchair users can access learning resources easily and safely	❏	❏
Work areas are adapted to an appropriate height for wheelchair users	❏	❏
All areas of the classroom are appropriately illuminated	❏	❏
The learning environment has appropriate acoustics to reduce background noise	❏	❏
The classroom in general is well organised to accommodate pupils with a disability	❏	❏

Access to information in a range of formats	YES	NO
Information is provided in alternative formats, (e.g. symbols, large print, audio, subtitles)	❏	❏
Pupils with a physical disability can access multi-media and mobile technology readily	❏	❏
You make effective use of the interactive whiteboard to produce written information in different formats	❏	❏
Pupils with a physical disability are able to record their responses in alternative ways to writing, as appropriate	❏	❏
Learning resources are clearly and appropriately labelled for pupils who have a sensory impairment	❏	❏

Figure 1.2 Meeting the Equality Act 2010 Duties to ensure access

Mobile Application to promote access to information

The Mobile Application is designed as a tool to turn messages from families, young people and practitioners into action. It is for use by parents and carers of disabled children and young people. The information gathered is then shared with professionals (e.g. doctors, nurses, teachers and the young person's employers).

Information entered can be in the form of text messages, photographs, films, resources or documents. Each of the sections in the Mobile Application has separate sharing permissions attached to it. Examples of useful sections in the Mobile Application include:

- information about conditions and disabilities;
- documents – assessments, e-books, reports, articles;
- local offer – links to all the local offers across England;
- contacts database;
- diary – to keep track of appointments;
- messaging.

More information is available at www.councilfordisabledchildren.org/earlysupport

Ofsted inspectors look at how teachers meet the Equality Act 2010 Duties and advance equality through:

- focusing on securing and maintaining excellent teaching, learning and assessment for all pupils;
- closing the gaps in achievement between different groups;
- ensuring pupils are free from bullying in all its forms;
- dealing with unacceptable behaviour and disruptions to learning; and
- building cohesive school communities, where all pupils can thrive.

Teachers may find useful Ofsted's document *Inspecting Equalities: Briefing for Section 5 Inspection* (Ofsted 2014d), available at www.ofsted.gov.uk, and the DfE's publication entitled *Equality Act 2010: Advice for Schools* (DfE 2013b), which can be downloaded from www.gov.uk/government/publications. The Equality and Human Rights Commission (EHRC) resources may also be of interest, such as *New Equality Act Guidance* (EHRC 2010a) and *Equality Act 2010: Education Providers – Schools' Guidance* (EHRC 2010b), available at www.equalityhumanrights.com/advice-and-guidance/new-equality-act-guidance/. The latter is currently being updated.

Ofsted inspections and SEND

Ofsted inspectors focus on four key areas in the inspection of schools and academies. These are:

1 the quality of leadership and management;

2 the behaviour and safety of pupils;

3 the quality of teaching;

4 the achievement of pupils.

In relation to SEND, Ofsted inspectors will check on:

- the aspirations for pupils with SEND;
- the motivation of pupils with SEND;
- the extent to which pupils with SEND use their initiative;
- whether pupils with SEND have sufficient opportunities to work independently during lessons;
- whether pupils with SEND have sufficient opportunities to learn collaboratively;
- how well the education provided for pupils with SEND meets their needs, particularly in relation to the outcomes and experiences for these pupils.

Ofsted identifies that the most important factor in determining the best outcomes for pupils with SEND is the quality of provision. Good outcomes for pupils with SEND are dependent on:

- good and outstanding teaching and learning;
- the close tracking and rigorous monitoring of pupil progress;
- high expectations;
- the promotion of independence;
- interventions put in place quickly and early.

Ofsted identified that the best learning for pupils with SEND occurs when teachers have:

- a detailed knowledge of the needs of the pupil with SEND;
- a thorough knowledge of appropriate teaching and learning strategies;
- good subject knowledge;
- a sound understanding of child development and how different learning difficulties and disabilities influence this.

The evidence Ofsted inspectors will seek in relation to SEND

Ofsted inspectors consider the extent to which the education provided meets the needs of pupils who have a disability, as defined by the Equality Act 2010, or who have SEN, or who are eligible for the pupil premium. In addition to undertaking lesson observations, inspectors will track a sample of pupils with SEND across the school for a day or half a day, to assess their experience.

The following list will act as an aide memoire for teachers as to what evidence Ofsted inspectors will look for when evaluating provision for pupils with SEND. Ofsted inspectors will:

- take into account the pupils' starting points in terms of their prior attainment and age;
- look at the progress made by pupils with SEND over the last three years, as well as within a lesson;

- judge the quality of teaching in relation to the impact it has on pupils' learning and progress over time;

- check to see that teaching strategies, homework, support and intervention match pupils' individual needs;

- consider how the additional interventions accessed by pupils with SEND link into other lessons (e.g. how they transfer this learning across the curriculum, and whether class and subject teachers know what the pupils have been studying in these sessions);

- gather evidence during lesson observations to check that pupils with SEND are engaged in lessons, acquire knowledge and learn well, and that teachers check pupils' understanding in lessons and make appropriate interventions;

- evaluate the use of, and contribution made by TAs, who should be clearly directed by teachers;

- check that teachers do not rely solely on TA information in relation to knowing how much progress pupils with SEND make;

- consider if TAs have sufficient subject knowledge to ensure that their input (e.g. the use of questioning) promotes pupils' thinking and learning

- check that teachers, TAs and other supporting adults are clear about what they want pupils with SEND to learn;

- consider if the lesson organisation and the physical learning environment ensure full access for pupils with a disability (if the teacher makes reasonable adjustments);

- evaluate whether teachers' expectations and aspirations for pupils with SEND are consistently high enough;

- expect teachers to be making use of the DfE's *Progression 2010–11* data sets and the Reporting and Analysis for Improvement through School (RAISEonline) Transition Matrices for judging the progress of pupils with SEND across a Key Stage, particularly in English and Maths.

While Ofsted inspectors do not advocate a particular method of teaching or show a preference towards a specific lesson structure, they will take note of the aspects of teaching that are effective, and identify ways in which teaching and learning can be improved. Ofsted see the most important role of teaching as being that which promotes learning and raises pupils' achievement.

Ofsted and teaching

Ofsted define teaching as including:

- teachers' planning and implementation of learning activities;
- the setting of appropriate homework;
- the marking, assessment and feedback that pupils receive on their work and learning;
- activities within and outside the classroom (i.e. the impact that additional support and interventions have on pupils' learning across the curriculum).

Where teaching is outstanding, pupils with SEND should make rapid and sustained progress.

Where teaching is good, pupils with SEND should make good progress and achieve well over time.

Ofsted see it as being the class and subject teachers' responsibility to ensure that work set is at the right level for pupils with SEND (i.e. matched to their reading age and ability).

Ofsted inspectors evaluating SEND pupils' learning over time

Ofsted inspectors will gather other evidence, in addition to undertaking lesson observations, to evaluate SEND pupils' learning over time. This includes:

- evidence from previous lesson observations, undertaken by the headteacher or other members of the senior leadership team;
- evidence gleaned from discussions with pupils about the work they have done and their experience of teaching and learning over longer periods;
- evidence from discussion about teaching and learning, and the effectiveness of interventions, with teachers, TAs and other staff;
- evidence on the views of pupils, parents and carers, and staff gathered from surveys and the Ofsted questionnaire;
- scrutiny of pupils' work across the curriculum, paying attention to:
  - how well and how frequently marking, assessment and testing are used to help teachers to improve pupils' learning;
  - the rigour of the moderation of teacher assessment, including P levels;
  - the level of challenge provided in the tasks set;
  - pupils' effort and success in completing their work;
  - the progress that pupils make in their written work over a period of time.

Teachers and trainee teachers will find it useful to download the following resources from the Ofsted website (www.ofsted.gov.uk):

- *School Inspection Handbook: Handbook for Inspecting Schools in England under Section 5 of the Education Act 2005* (Ofsted 2014a);
- *The Framework for School Inspection: The Framework for Inspecting Schools in England under Section 5 of the Education Act 2005* (Ofsted 2014b);
- *Subsidiary Guidance: Supporting the Inspection of Maintained Schools and Academies* (Ofsted 2014c).

Teachers' professional development for SEND

The draft 2014 *SEND Code of Practice* sees teachers securing SEND expertise at three different levels, through professional development:

1 **awareness** – giving a basic awareness of a particular type of SEN to all staff, who are likely to come into contact with a pupil with that type of SEN;

2 **enhanced** – professional development on how to adapt teaching and learning to meet a particular type of SEN, for those class and subject teachers working directly with the pupil on a regular basis;

3 specialist – in-depth training about a particular type of SEN, for staff who will be advising and supporting those with enhanced-level skills and knowledge.

(DfE 2014g: 56–57)

Training and continuing professional development in SEND for teachers, trainees and NQTs can be accessed in a number of ways:

- attending in-house whole-school in-service education and training (INSET) sessions delivered by the SENCO or an external professional, and 'drop-in' SEND sessions offered by the SENCO in school;

- attending workshops and seminars on a range of topics related to SEND at a local teaching school who have a specialism in SEND;

- accessing individual coaching or mentoring sessions, as appropriate, from another colleague in or beyond the school (e.g. a SENCO, an SLE in SEND or a SEND consultant);

- attending any LA SEND training events;

- attending external conferences and training days organised and run by private training providers and national organisations, such as the National Association for Special Educational Needs (nasen);

- work shadowing another teacher or SENCO to observe them teaching a diversity of pupils with SEND;

- visiting other local schools with a resourced provision for SEND, including special schools, to observe teaching and discuss assessment, curriculum access and useful teaching resources;

- accessing online multi-media SEND training resources, and working on these over time.

Teachers and trainee teachers can access a range of DfE SEND online modules – for example, the Inclusion Development Programme (IDP) resources, and the DfE multi-media Advanced training materials for autism; dyslexia; speech, language and communication; emotional, social and behavioural difficulties; and moderate learning difficulties.

There are also online DfE multi-media training resources available on complex needs, which can be of value where there are pupils with severe learning difficulties (SLD) being taught in the mainstream classroom. These training resources are available to download or access online at:

- www.idponline.org.uk;

- www.advanced-training.org.uk and www.complexneeds.org.uk;

- www.education.gov.uk.

The nasen website also offers phase-specific training toolkits for SEND entitled *A Whole School Approach to Improving Access, Participation and Achievement* that can be accessed at www.nasentraining.org.uk/primary-training/ (for the Primary phase toolkit) and www.nasentraining.org.uk/training-pack/ (for the Secondary phase toolkit).

An overview of the SEND training resources for teachers and trainees

The IDP

This bank of online resources, which is comprised of downloadable materials and video clips and which was produced by the previous Labour government to support their SEND strategy Removing Barriers to Achievement, was designed to enable teachers to improve outcomes for pupils with SEND. The resources are organised by phase – Early Years, Primary and Secondary – and they cover the following SEND aspects:

- BESD;
- autism spectrum;
- speech, language and communication needs (SLCN);
- dyslexia.

Some of the documentary materials with these online SEND modules can support further activities for professional development, particularly for trainees and NQTs.

A Whole School Approach to Improving Access, Participation and Achievement

Each Primary and Secondary phase toolkit has four training modules, which the SENCO can use to develop future tailored training sessions with groups of staff. The four modules cover:

1 inclusive teaching and learning;
2 tracking progress;
3 working with others;
4 communication with pupils.

Each module is comprised of a series of Activity and Information Sheets, which the SENCO may wish to use to support the other online SEND training resources.

The advanced training materials for autism; dyslexia; speech, language and communication; emotional, social and behavioural difficulties; and moderate learning difficulties

These phase-specific SEND resources, comprised of five modules (one for each area of SEND), feature reading-based materials and practical training tasks, with a range of audio and video clips to support study. They are designed to improve teachers' knowledge, skills and understanding about each area of SEND, as well as helping school staff to raise the achievement of pupils with SEND.

Training materials for teachers of learners with SLD

These training resources can be useful for those working or training in a special school setting. However, children with SLD, such as Down's Syndrome, may be accessing learning in a mainstream setting, either full time or part time as dual-placement pupils. Teachers will need to select which of the 16 modules would be appropriate to access, particularly if they are teaching a pupil with SLD. The modules cover four broad subject areas:

1 the context of specialist teaching;

2 specialist teaching strategies;

3 specialist teaching procedure;

4 collaboration and leadership.

This is another excellent set of SEND training resources, like the Advanced training materials, which includes video clips to illustrate best practice in the classroom. Subject areas 2 and 3 would be the most useful, as these focus on planning, curriculum access, AfL and communication.

The concept, use and impact of the pupil premium

The pupil premium was introduced by the coalition government in April 2011. This additional funding targets extra support for looked after children (LAC), who have been looked after continuously for more than six months; for those on free school meals (FSM) from low-income families, including those who have been eligible for FSM at any point in the past six years; and for children with a parent or carer in the armed forces, from Reception to Year 11. The extra pupil premium funding for schools is designed to help to narrow the attainment gap between pupils from disadvantaged and more affluent backgrounds, some of whom may have SEND. The coalition government announced in March 2014 that an early years pupil premium is to be introduced in 2015. This will enable early years providers to give more support and help to those young children from the most disadvantaged backgrounds.

Reporting on the use of the pupil premium

It is up to schools to decide how they spend the pupil premium. They are accountable for their use of the funding and they have to publish information online about their annual pupil premium allocation and how they spent it, year on year. Schools must also indicate what impact the extra funding has had on the learning, progress and attainment of pupil premium children. During school inspections, Ofsted wants to know why the school has decided to spend the pupil premium in the way it has. Inspectors evaluate the performance of pupil premium children in English and Maths by considering average points scores in national assessments at the end of Key Stage 2 and in GCSEs at the end of Key Stage 4. Where a gap is identified between the performance of pupils supported through the pupil premium and all others in the school, it is reported whether this is narrowing.

How schools used the pupil premium

From April 2011, when the pupil premium was first introduced, schools had little if any guidance from the DfE on how best to use this additional funding. Therefore, schools went for a fairly narrow menu of support and interventions. These included:

- creating smaller classes;
- providing one-to-one tuition;
- introducing ability grouping;
- recruiting extra TAs;
- extending the school day to fit in after-school activities.

In 2012, Ofsted undertook its first review of how schools were using the pupil premium to raise the achievement of disadvantaged pupils. The most common uses for the pupil premium at that time were to pay for TAs to deliver in-class support or small-group time-limited interventions in literacy and/or numeracy, or for existing or new well-qualified or specialist teachers to deliver focused support in English and/ or Maths, or to help to reduce class sizes, or to deliver out-of-hours learning. Other schools had used the pupil premium money to fund support workers, learning mentors, parent support workers, behaviour support workers and counsellors to address pupil well-being. Schools had also used the additional money to fund extra-curricular activities, educational trips and residential visits for disadvantaged pupils, to pay for school uniform and to supply basic equipment to support pupils' learning. Some secondary schools funded summer schools from the pupil premium money.

In 2013, Ofsted undertook a follow-up review of the pupil premium, which once again focused on how schools were using the pupil premium to maximise achievement. This report was more sharply focused, as it offered several case studies as evidence of good practice (i.e. of what was working well).

Implications for teachers

Class and subject teachers need to:

- know which pupils are eligible for the pupil premium in the classes they teach;
- ensure that these pupils benefit from consistently high-quality teaching;
- track pupil premium children's progress regularly each term to check whether additional support and interventions are working, and make any necessary adjustments to teaching and support;
- deploy TAs effectively to ensure that they promote and extend pupil premium children's learning;
- systematically give pupil premium children useful diagnostic feedback on their work, indicating ways in which they could improve it;
- monitor the attendance, punctuality and behaviour of pupil premium children, and ensure that they catch up on work missed.

In January 2013, Ofsted published *The Pupil Premium: Analysis and Challenge Tools for Schools* (Ofsted 2013b) which accompanied the report *The Pupil Premium: How Schools Are Spending the Funding Successfully to Maximise Achievement* (Ofsted 2013a) This Ofsted toolkit enables teachers to analyse where there are gaps in achievement between pupils who are eligible for the pupil premium and those who are not, and to plan the subsequent action they need to take. The self-review questions on pp. 13–15 of the toolkit document are worth considering. Both the toolkit and the pupil premium report can be downloaded from www.ofsted.gov.uk.

What works best in raising the achievement of those on the pupil premium

Teachers may find Table 1.2 of interest, as this identifies which additional interventions and support are the most effective and have the greatest impact. It is rooted in evidence-based practice, undertaken by Durham University and the Education

Table 1.2

Pupil premium approaches and their impact

Approach	Potential gain	Cost	Impact
After-school programmes	2 months	££££	Low impact for a high cost
Arts participation	2 months	££	Low impact for a low cost
Aspiration interventions	0 months	£££	Very low or no impact for a moderate cost
Behaviour interventions	4 months	£££	Moderate impact for a very high cost
Block scheduling	0 months	£	Very low or no impact for a very low or no cost
Collaborative learning	5 months	£	Moderate impact for a very low cost
Digital technology	4 months	££££	Moderate impact for a high cost
Early years intervention	6 months	£££££	High impact for a very high cost
Extended school time	2 months	£££	Low impact for a moderate cost
Feedback	8 months	££	High impact for a low cost
Homework (Primary)	1 month	£	Low impact for low or no cost
Homework (Secondary)	5 months	£	Moderate impact for a very low or no cost
Individualised instruction	2 months	£	Low impact for a low cost
Learning styles	2 months	£	Low impact for a very low cost
Mastery learning	5 months	££	Moderate impact for a low cost
Mentoring	1 month	£££	Low impact for a moderate cost
Meta-cognition and self-regulation	8 months	££	High impact for a low cost
One-to-one tuition	5 months	££££	Moderate impact for a high cost
Oral language interventions	5 months	££	Moderate impact for a low cost
Outdoor adventure learning	3 months	£££	Moderate impact for a moderate cost
Parental/carer involvement	3 months	£££	Moderate impact for a moderate cost
Peer tutoring	6 months	££	High impact for a low cost
Performance pay	0 months	££	Very low or no impact for a low cost
Phonics	4 months	£	Moderate impact for a very low cost
Physical environment	0 months	££	Very low or no impact for a low cost
Reducing class size	3 months	£££££	Low impact for a very high cost
Repeating a year	− 4 months	£££££	Negative impact for a very high cost
School uniform	0 months	£	Very low or no impact for a very low cost
Setting or streaming	−1 month	£	Negative impact for a very low or no cost
Small-group tuition	4 months	£££	Moderate impact for a moderate cost
Social and emotional learning	4 months	£	Moderate impact for a very low cost
Sports participation	2 months	£££	Moderate impact for a moderate cost
Summer schools	3 months	£££	Moderate impact for a moderate cost
Teaching assistants	1 month	££££	Low impact for a high cost

(Source: The Sutton Trust–EEF 2012: 2; Higgins et al. 2014: 2)

Endowment Foundation (EEF) on behalf of the Sutton Trust. The interactive *Teaching and Learning Toolkit* (The Sutton Trust–EEF 2012; Higgins *et al.* 2014) can be viewed and downloaded from www.educationendowmentfoundation.org.uk/toolkit/.

In summary, the most effective provision, having the best impact, included:

- teaching through the eyes of children;
- giving pupils regular constructive feedback on their learning;
- encouraging pupils to self-review their learning;
- including meta-cognition and self-regulation as part of everyday high-quality teaching and learning (pupils talking about learning, learning about learning and thinking about thinking);
- encouraging pupils to use thinking skills, mind mapping and open questioning and giving them sufficient thinking time;
- encouraging pupils to use 'pole bridging' (explaining to other peers what they did to learn something or to solve a problem);
- using visual prompts and displays to promote learning;
- giving pupils breaks between learning activities;
- peer tutoring;
- giving pupils collaborative learning opportunities;
- offering phonics interventions for those who require catch-up.

Teachers and trainee teachers will notice that, apart from phonics, it is the features of high-quality teaching and learning, as part of everyday classroom practice, that have the greatest impact for those on the pupil premium.

Questions for reflection

1 What will be your greatest challenge in meeting the draft 2014 SEND Code of Practice expectation of every teacher being responsible for pupils with SEND, and how will you address this?

2 Having viewed the online SEND training resources from the DfE and nasen, which areas of SEND do you feel you require further information about, and how will you go about gaining this knowledge?

3 In readiness for a forthcoming Ofsted inspection, what evidence will you bring together in one place to demonstrate the reasonable adjustments made to ensure that pupils with SEND have access to the curriculum, to the physical learning environment and to information in different formats, as appropriate?

4 In light of the principles that underpin the draft 2014 SEND Code of Practice, which one is a top priority for you to develop your understanding further, in order to effectively meet the needs of pupils with SEND?

5 The senior leader responsible for overseeing pupil premium funding has asked you to present evidence as to how you have made a difference to the outcomes for the pupil premium children you teach. Describe the evidence you will present.

Promoting good progress and outcomes for pupils with SEND

This chapter covers:

- Teacher accountability for SEND pupils' attainment, progress and outcomes
- Making best use of the DfE guidance on Progression
- SEN Support: a graduated approach to ensuring the progress of pupils with SEND
- The brain, memory and their influence on SEND pupils' learning and progress
- Meta-cognition and self-regulation to improve SEND pupils' learning and progress
- Supporting pupils with SEND to become independent learners
- Setting relevant homework to enhance SEND pupils' learning and progress

Teacher accountability for SEND pupils' attainment, progress and outcomes

The DfE facts and figures about SEN, taken from the School Census return for the academic year 2012–13, indicate that:

- At Key Stage 2, only 14 per cent of pupils with statements of SEN achieved the expected level in both English and Maths, compared to 88 per cent of pupils without SEN.
- At Key Stage 4, only 9.5 per cent of pupils with statements of SEN achieved a Level 2 qualification including English and Maths, compared to 70.4 per cent of pupils without SEN.
- Young people with SEN are more than twice as likely to be not in education, employment or training (NEET). (DfE 2014l: 6–8)

Clearly, these statistics relating to the achievement and progress of pupils with SEN are a cause for concern, especially where they have made less than the expected rate of progress over time.

The draft 2014 *SEND Code of Practice (0 to 25)*, in Chapter 6, helpfully defines what 'making less than expected progress' constitutes:

Class and subject teachers, supported by the senior leadership team, should make regular assessments of progress for all pupils. These should seek to identify pupils making less than expected progress given their age and individual circumstances. This can be characterised by progress that:

- is significantly slower than that of their peers starting from the same baseline;
- fails to match or better the child's previous rate of progress;
- fails to close the attainment gap between the child and their peers;
- widens the attainment gap.

(DfE 2014g: 6.14)

Chapter 6 of the draft 2014 *SEND Code of Practice* opens with the following comment:

All children and young people are entitled to an education that enables them to make progress so that they:

- achieve their best;
- become confident individuals living fulfilling lives; and
- make a successful transition into adulthood, whether into employment, further or higher education or training.

(DfE 2014g: 6.1)

Later in the same chapter, the draft 2014 *SEND Code of Practice* emphasises that 'Teachers are responsible and accountable for the progress and development of the pupils in their class, including where pupils access support from teaching assistants or specialist staff' (DfE 2014g: 6.33).

However, the draft 2014 *SEND Code of Practice* does give a 'health' warning about progress and SEND, when it states that:

Slow progress and low attainment do not necessarily mean that a child has SEN and should not automatically lead to a pupil being recorded as having SEN . . . Some learning difficulties and disabilities occur across the range of cognitive ability.

(DfE 2014g: 6.20)

If pupils make less than expected progress, the draft 2014 *SEND Code of Practice* states that:

The first response to such progress should be high quality teaching targeted at their areas of weakness. Where progress continues to be less than expected the class or subject teacher, working with the SENCO, should assess whether the child has SEN.

(DfE 2014g: 6.16)

The draft 2014 *SEND Code of Practice* acknowledges that progress relates not only to attainment, but also to a pupil's wider development or social needs, in order to enable them to make a smooth transition into adult life. Ofsted expects all teachers to show evidence of the progress made by pupils with SEND whom they teach. Ofsted's *Subsidiary Guidance: Supporting the Inspection of Maintained Schools and Academies* (April 2014) provides further guidance on how they make judgements about the progress made by pupils with SEND. This document can be downloaded from www.ofsted.gov.uk.

The Inclusion section of the new national curriculum, implemented from September 2014, emphasises that teachers should set high expectations for every pupil, irrespective of their prior attainment. It goes on to state that:

> Teachers . . . have an even greater obligation to plan lessons for pupils who have low levels of attainment or come from disadvantaged backgrounds. Lessons should be planned to ensure that there are no barriers to every pupil achieving.
>
> (DfE 2013h: 9)

Making best use of the DfE guidance on Progression

There is no single definition of what 'good progress' looks like for pupils with SEND. However, in its updated *Progression 2010–11* guidance (DfE 2010b), the DfE clarified three key principles that, taken together, lead to pupils with SEND making good progress:

1 **High expectations are key to securing good progress.** Both are facilitated by teachers promoting equality of opportunity for pupils with SEND as learners in the inclusive classroom, through the removal or minimisation of barriers to learning and participation. Some pupils with SEND who have more complex learning difficulties (e.g. profound and multiple learning difficulties (PMLD), SLD) may make slower progress because they need time to consolidate and generalise newly acquired skills within a single curriculum level. This smaller-stepped progress is also referred to as lateral or horizontal progress.

2 **Accurate assessment is essential to securing and measuring pupil progress.** With the government's recent reforms to the curriculum and assessment, effective moderation of teacher assessment is important in enabling class and subject teachers to develop a shared understanding and to make well-founded and consistent 'best-fit' judgements about the progress of pupils with SEND, across the curriculum. The professional dialogue that supports the moderation and standardisation of teacher assessment contributes greatly to the improvement of teaching and learning for pupils with SEND.

3 **Age and prior attainment are the starting points for developing expectations of pupil progress.** The prior attainment of pupils with SEND reflects not only the learning difficulties they have, but also how well they have been taught and progressed. Knowing where these pupils are in their learning helps class and subject teachers to set appropriate targets and have realistic expectations. Having a clear understanding of SEND pupils' needs in respect of their age is critical to delivering personalised and differentiated high-quality teaching because it informs:

- the range of strategies teachers use;
- the nature of the provision;
- the nature of the reasonable adjustments required to remove or minimise barriers to learning.

The DfE Progression guidance identifies that the best predictor of future SEND pupil attainment is past performance, plus a degree of challenge, as evidenced in the national P level data sets upper quartile outcomes, offered in Appendix D of the DfE's

Progression 2010–11 document (DfE 2010b). However, teachers need to be mindful that these data sets are based on the old P level and national curriculum point scores, and therefore should be used with caution, as they will not necessarily provide an up-to-date benchmark for comparison with SEND pupil achievement from 2014 onwards, which will be aligned to the new 2014 national curriculum, and expressed as scaled scores rather than as levels.

SEN Support: a graduated approach to ensuring the progress of pupils with SEND

The graduated approach offers class and subject teachers a four-part cycle to providing SEN Support for those pupils identified with SEND who do not require or already have an EHC plan. The draft 2014 *SEND Code of Practice* confirms that the graduated approach 'draws on more detailed approaches, more frequent review and more specialist expertise in successive cycles in order to match interventions to the SEN of children and young people' (DfE 2014g: 6.40). The SENCO in the education setting will be able to offer further advice and guidance to class and subject teachers on how to put the graduated approach into practice.

The four parts of the graduated approach are as follows:

1 Assess: At this first stage in the cycle, the class or subject teacher, in partnership with the SENCO, carries out a clear analysis of the pupil's needs, which draws on:

- the teacher's assessment and experience of teaching and working with the pupil;
- the pupil's previous progress and attainment, including information from the school's own core approach to pupil progress, attainment and behaviour;
- other subject teachers' assessments, where relevant;
- the individual pupil's development in comparison to their peers and national data;
- the views and experiences of the pupil's parents or carers;
- the pupil's own views;
- any advice and evidence from external support services, where appropriate.

Assessment is reviewed every term, by the class or subject teacher. This regular, ongoing assessment and review of progress ensures that the support and interventions put in place are matched to the pupil's needs, and any barriers to learning and participation are identified and overcome.

2 Plan: The parents or carers of the pupil with SEND are formally notified that their child will be receiving SEN Support on the graduated approach. In discussion with the parents or carers and the pupil, the class or subject teacher and the SENCO agree the adjustments, interventions and support to be put in place, the expected impact on the pupil's progress, development or behaviour, and the date for the review.

All the teachers and support staff who work with the pupil are made aware of the pupil's needs, the expected outcomes, the support being provided, and the most effective teaching strategies and support for learning approaches to use. All of this information is recorded on the education setting's information system.

The support and intervention provided is delivered by staff with the skills and relevant knowledge, and is based on robust evidence of what works best in relation to the effectiveness of the particular additional support and interventions being delivered. The parents or carers are involved in the planned support and interventions, in respect of how they can follow up with reinforcement and contributions at home.

3 Do: The class or subject teacher remains responsible for working with the pupil on a daily basis, even when an intervention involves small-group or individual teaching away from the main class or subject teacher. The class or subject teacher works closely with the TA or specialist staff, to plan and assess the impact of support and interventions and how they can be linked to classroom teaching. The SENCO supports the class or subject teacher in the further assessment of the pupil's particular strengths and weaknesses, in problem solving and in advising on the effective implementation of support.

4 Review: The effectiveness of the support and interventions and their impact on the pupil's progress is reviewed in line with the agreed date. The impact and quality of the support and interventions are evaluated, along with the views of the pupil and their parents or carers. This information is fed back into the analysis of the pupil's needs. The class or subject teacher, working with the SENCO, revises the support in light of the pupil's progress and development, deciding on any changes to the support and outcomes, in consultation with the parents or carers and the pupil.

The involvement of specialists in the graduated approach

Where a pupil on SEN Support continues to make less than expected progress, despite evidence-based support and interventions being matched to the pupil's particular needs, specialists from within and beyond the education setting become involved. These specialists from education, health or social care services can include an educational psychologist, a social worker, a Child and Adolescent Mental Health Service (CAMHS) worker, a specialist teacher (e.g. a teacher of the hearing impaired), or a physiotherapist, occupational therapist or a speech and language therapist. The draft 2014 *SEND Code of Practice* comments:

> A school should always involve a specialist where a pupil continues to make little or no progress over a sustained period or where they continue to work at levels substantially below those expected of pupils of a similar age despite evidence-based SEN support delivered by appropriately trained staff.
>
> (DfE 2014g: 6.53)

The SENCO and class or subject teacher, together with the specialists and the pupil's parents or carers, agree upon the evidence-based effective teaching approaches and the appropriate specialist equipment, strategies and interventions to put in place to further support the pupil's progress.

The brain, memory and their influence on SEND pupils' learning and progress

The brain and learning

The brain functions best when it is exposed to the optimum conditions for learning, which include:

- exercise through brain breaks which help the supply of oxygen and glucose to reach the brain;
- regular access to drinking water;
- a relaxed, calm learning environment free from emotional stress;
- a good supply of fish oils (Omega 3) and iron- and zinc-rich foods such as green leaf vegetables, fruit, nuts, fish and vegetable oil.

Facts about the brain

- At birth, most children have 100 billion active brain nerve cells.
- By eight months, a baby's brain has 1,000 trillion connections.
- During the first three years of a child's life, the foundations of thinking, language, vision, attitudes and aptitudes are laid down.
- The brain's cerebral cortex grows most rapidly in the first ten years of a child's life.
- By ten years of age in the average child, half of the 1,000 trillion connections have died off.
- 50 per cent of an individual's ability to learn is developed in the first four years of life. Another 30 per cent of that ability is developed by the age of eight, and the final 20 per cent is developed by the age of seventeen.
- The adult brain weighs about 3 lbs.
- The brain is not designed to be constantly attentive.
- Smoking, alcohol and drugs in excess severely affect the growth and effectiveness of the brain.

The differences between male and female brains

It is useful for teachers to be aware of the differences between male and female brains, and to take account of these when tailoring and delivering high-quality teaching. Teachers need to engage pupils with SEND in learning activities that use both sides of the brain, even though traditionally the national curriculum has been biased towards left brain activities. Table 2.1 outlines the differences between the male and female brain and Figure 2.1 lists the left and right brain hemisphere characteristics.

Brain physiology

- The **corpus callosum**, which links both sides of the brain together, allows the left and right hemispheres of the brain to communicate and exchange information.
- The **prefrontal cortex** deals with thinking and emotions.

Table 2.1

Differences between the male and female brain

Male brain	Female brain
– Males develop the right side of their brain faster than females, which results in them having better visual, spatial, logical and perceptual skills than females.	– Females develop the left side of their brain more rapidly than boys, which results in them speaking sooner, reading earlier and learning a foreign language more quickly than males.
– The male brain has fewer connecting fibres between the left and right sides and is a more compartmentalised brain, which accounts for why males find it difficult to multi-task, unlike females.	– Baby girls generally develop their corpus callosum (the bundle of nerve fibres connecting the left and right sides of the brain together) earlier than boys, which accounts for why girls acquire language skills before boys.
– The male brain is 9 per cent physically bigger than the female brain, but this does not make males cleverer than females, as both sexes have the same number of brain cells.	– The corpus callosum is generally thicker in baby girls than in baby boys, which results in females having up to 30 per cent more connections between the two sides of the brain than males.
– The right side of the male brain is larger than the left side.	– The left side of the female brain is larger than the right side.
– Males favour the right ear for listening.	– Females listen with both ears.
– The male brain shrinks by 20 per cent by the age of 50.	– The female brain does not shrink with age.
– Males are three times more likely to be dyslexic than females.	
– Males are more frequently left-handed than females.	
– Males have a shorter attention span than females.	

LEFT HEMISPHERE	RIGHT HEMISPHERE
Female	Male
Academic brain	Creative brain
Right side of body	Left side of body
Enjoys structured tasks	Enjoys open-ended tasks and self selected tasks
Clear instructions	
Written information	Follows hunches and is impulsive
Mathematical formula	Artistic
Numbers	Visual
Judgement of quantity	Pictures and images
Logical	Imaginative
Verbal	Perceptive
Words	Ideas
Phonetic reading	Enjoys sport
Spelling	Forms and patterns
Writing	Dimension
Language	Spatial manipulation
Facts	Daydreaming
Unrelated factual information	Visioning
Deduction	Fantasy
Analysis	Rhyme
Practical	Rhythm
Order	Musical
Sequence	Musical appreciation
Words of a song	Tune of a song
Lineal	Whole language reader
Sees fine detail	Sees the big picture
Learning the parts to whole	Learns the whole first then the parts

Figure 2.1 Left and right brain hemisphere characteristics

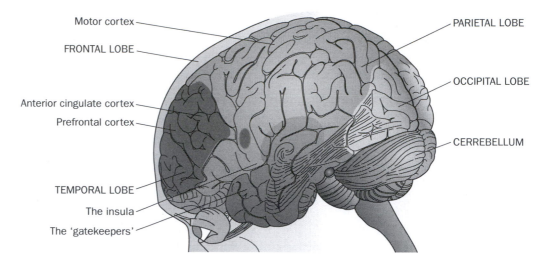

Figure 2.2 The component parts of the brain

- The **anterior cingulate cortex** weighs up options, makes decisions and is the 'worry' centre.
- The **motor cortex** controls activity.
- The **temporal lobe** is the speech centre of the brain.
- The **insula** is the centre that processes gut feelings.
- The **parietal lobe** handles spatial ability.
- The **occipital lobe** is the visual centre of the brain.
- The **cerebellum** is the 'little brain' that plays a key part in adjusting posture and balance.
- The **'gatekeepers'** – three in total: the **amygdala**, the **hippocampus** and the **caudate nucleus** – relay important messages to the brain and are responsible for instinct and memory.

Figure 2.2 illustrates the component parts of the brain.

The brain and dyslexia

A child who is born with dyslexia has both sides of the brain equally developed, resulting in less efficient nerve fibres between the right and left sides of the brain. This is different to non-dyslexic children, whose left side of the brain (which develops language skills) is more developed than the right side of the brain. This factor accounts for why dyslexic children, particularly boys, have great difficulty in processing information and struggle to acquire the language skills of reading, spelling and writing, and why they also experience difficulties with memory, coordination, time management, concentration and attention to task. Pupils with dyslexia find it difficult to transfer what they have learned to new situations, because they struggle with monitoring and reflecting upon their own learning.

Therefore, it is really important that pupils with dyslexia have access to the use of multi-sensory learning approaches (e.g. visual, auditory and kinaesthetic (VAK)), both in lessons and when completing homework tasks. Class and subject teachers also need to guide and support pupils with dyslexia in how to use previous learning, by asking them the question 'How do you know this?' throughout the learning experience, in order to help them to develop their meta-cognitive learning competencies and to improve their transfer of learning.

Facts about learning and the memory

- On average, pupils remember:
  - 20 per cent of what is read;
  - 30 per cent of what is heard;
  - 40 per cent of what is seen displayed;
  - 50 per cent of what is said or explained to others;
  - 60 per cent of what is done in practical work;
  - 90 per cent if all of the above multi-sensory methods are used in learning.
- 80 per cent of new knowledge is lost within 24 hours, without a review of learning.

A learner's maximum concentration span on average is two minutes in excess of their chronological age, in minutes. For example:

- A six-year-old's maximum time on task is 6 minutes with a 2–3-minute break from task.
- A ten-year-old's maximum time on task is 12 minutes with a 2–5-minute break from task.
- An eleven to twelve-year-old's maximum time on task is 15 minutes with a 2–5-minute break from task.
- A fifteen to sixteen-year-old's maximum time on task is 20 minutes with a 2–5-minute break from task.
- An adult's maximum time on task is 20–25 minutes with a 2–5-minute break from task.

Types of memory and learning

There is no one single part of the brain specifically used to store a pupil's memories. There are five types of memory, which are as follows:

1 **Working memory:** This is extremely short (i.e. only a few seconds long). It is situated in the prefrontal and parietal cortices of the brain.

2 **Implicit memory:** This is when a pupil remembers how to do a task after a lengthy break in time (e.g. riding a bicycle again, after not cycling for a number of years). This type of memory is divided into 'reflexive' and 'procedural', and is stored in the cerebellum.

3 **Remote memory:** This is when a pupil remembers general knowledge information and trivia that they have gathered over a number of years. This type of memory is spread around the neocortex.

4 **Episodic memory:** This is when a pupil remembers specific personal experiences, such as a family holiday, a birthday or another family event. This type of memory is stored in the hippocampus.

5 Semantic memory: This type of memory entails the retention of the meaning of words and symbols, people, films, videos and diagrams, including information from the internet. It is created in the hippocampus and is stored in the angular gyrus area of the brain.

Class and subject teachers, however, are likely to see the following terms related to a child's memory, featured in the reports of educational psychologists.

- **Working memory:** This refers to the retention of information in short-term (temporary) storage while processing incoming information and retrieving information from long-term storage. Short-term storage within this working memory model refers to holding information in the memory for 'seconds' before it fades away or is discarded. The average individual cannot hold more than six or seven units of information in short-term memory.

  If a pupil is distracted or interrupted while using working memory, the process is halted and they are unable to resume from where they were interrupted, and thus they have to start the task from the beginning again. For example, in a class of 30 seven-year-olds, three children are likely to have the working memory capacity of a four-year-old, and three pupils are likely to have the working memory capacity of a ten-year-old. Pupils with a relatively poor working memory tend to perform below average (e.g. those with SLD, specific learning difficulties (SpLD) or moderate learning difficulties (MLD)).

  Working memory ability is a better predictor of achievement than short-term memory. For example, a pupil aged ten with working memory difficulties will struggle to hold three or more pieces of information in short-term storage.

- **Short-term memory:** This refers to the storage of information for a matter of seconds, without having to manipulate it in any way. If a pupil has to manipulate what they are holding in short-term memory to complete a task, or while doing something else at the same time, they are using working memory. Some pupils need a lot of repetition at regular intervals before some information is transferred to the long-term memory store. Other pupils will need much less repetition and rehearsal. Too much rehearsal, however, can disrupt a pupil's working memory.

- **Long-term memory:** This refers to the permanent storage of knowledge in memory stores located in various parts of the brain. Retrieval from long-term memory is aided by meaning. Unless meaning is attached to new learning, retrieval will be difficult.

Some pupils with SEND have memory problems that make learning more difficult. Teachers need to be aware that tasks that place demands on various aspects of memory can make a pupil's learning difficulties worse, causing a barrier to learning and progress. For example, when a teacher asks a pupil to repeat a simple number sequence, the pupil uses short-term memory. When a teacher presents a pupil with a simple number sequence and asks them to repeat it backwards, this involves working memory.

Signs that a pupil may have working memory difficulties

Class and subject teachers need to look out for pupils displaying the following behaviours:

- incomplete recall;
- failure to follow instructions;
- difficulty keeping their place in a text;
- abandoning the task and giving up easily;
- poorly organised;
- inattentive, and missing what the teacher has said.

It is not unusual for a pupil with SEND to be able to remember and recall what they did on a favourite holiday a couple of years ago, but be unable to remember a concept or a fact that they came across two days ago in a lesson. The strength of a memory, and the ease with which it is retrieved by a pupil with SEND, is dependent on the strength and processing of the initial input. That factor is why it is so important for teachers to use multi-sensory teaching and learning approaches (VAK).

Top tips to improve pupils' memory

Class and subject teachers may find the following strategies and approaches helpful in supporting memory recall among pupils with SEND:

- Chunk similar pieces of information together in one group, category or set to help pupils to remember more easily.
- Help pupils to link together (associate) and connect information on a topic through VAK approaches, using all the senses, and/or movement (actions and gestures) to link memories.
- Make use of mnemonics, jingles and rhymes to help pupils to remember key terms, spell a word correctly or remember the order or components of something (e.g. the colours of the rainbow).
- Use humorous images to help pupils to remember something important.
- Use symbols to help pupils to remember something vividly.
- Use colour coding (e.g. highlighter pens) to support pupils' visual memory.
- Make things bigger, brighter or louder, where appropriate, to help pupils to form powerful long-term memories.
- Encourage pupils to produce and make use of a mind map to prompt their memory and prior learning on a particular topic or subject. Mind maps are very useful for creating and organising a pupil's ideas, and for helping them to memorise information, particularly when pictures and graphics are incorporated with the text.
- Repeat key information in a range of different ways (e.g. use memory prompt cards, visuals, key headings) to help pupils to over-learn and prompt memory recall.
- Make use of role play to help pupils to understand and retain information (e.g. drama activities, 'hot seating').
- Improve pupils' understanding of a topic or subject by using key questions (e.g. 'Why?', 'What?', 'When?', 'Where?', 'How?'). Understanding is the key to the efficient use of memory, and comes before memory retention.

Strategies teachers can use to reduce memory overload

- Use shorter sentences.
- Give instructions one step at a time, and accompany them with visuals.
- Provide meaningful associations.
- Break down tasks into smaller component parts.
- Pair up a pupil with poor working memory with another peer with good memory skills.
- Encourage the use of memory aids and prompts (e.g. number lines, number squares, word banks).
- Encourage pupils with poor working memory to make use of a learning log, memory diary or visual timetable.
- Allow extra thinking time when asking pupils with poor working memory a question that requires information recall.

Meta-cognition and self-regulation to improve SEND pupils' learning and progress

The concepts of meta-cognition and self-regulation

The concept meta-cognition refers to 'learning to learn', 'knowing about knowing' and 'thinking about thinking'. It refers to a pupil's awareness of their own knowledge; what they do and do not know; their ability to understand, control and manipulate their own cognitive processes. It includes when and where to use particular meta-cognitive skills and strategies to promote learning and solve problems.

Self-regulation refers to pupils managing their own motivation towards learning, and maintaining motivation in order to complete a given task, which is a meta-cognitive skill. Self-regulation also refers to the cognitive aspects of thinking and reasoning – in other words, being able to use the right approaches, and to modify learning strategies and skills based on their awareness of effectiveness.

In order to enable pupils to think more explicitly about their learning, class and subject teachers need to teach pupils specific strategies (meta-cognitive skills) to help them to set goals, monitor, self-assess and evaluate their own learning.

The components of meta-cognition

Meta-cognition is classified into three components. These are:

1 **Meta-cognitive knowledge** (also referred to as **meta-cognitive awareness**) – this is what pupils know about themselves and others as cognitive processors.

2 **Meta-cognitive regulation** – this is the regulation of cognition and learning experiences through a set of activities that help the pupil to control their learning (self-regulation).

3 **Meta-cognitive experiences** – this refers to those experiences that have something to do with the current, ongoing cognitive endeavour.

Meta-cognitive skills

Meta-cognitive skills are associated with an understanding of how learning occurs (i.e. pupils being able to talk about learning and how they learn best, and identifying other people who help them to learn). Usually, when pupils are asked by teachers to describe how they learn, they will refer to learning by listening, remembering, making notes, learning by doing, guessing or applying previous learnt knowledge.

Meta-cognition involves a number of skills, which include:

- controlling the process of thinking;
- planning the way to approach a learning task;
- monitoring comprehension;
- making judgements about the strength of memories;
- evaluating the progress towards the completion of a task;
- self-assessing learning.

Strategies that promote meta-cognition

Meta-cognition plays a crucial role in successful learning, and this is why it is important for teachers to equip pupils of all abilities with the necessary meta-cognitive skills.

Listed below are some of the most effective teaching strategies for promoting meta-cognition:

- modelling and demonstrating a range of meta-cognitive skills;
- encouraging other pupils proficient in using and applying meta-cognitive skills to act as mentors to pupils with SEND, enabling them to develop such skills;
- encouraging pupils to self-question (e.g. to ask themselves 'What do I already know about this topic?' or 'How have I solved problems like this before?');
- encouraging pupils to think aloud when undertaking a task or solving a problem;
- encouraging pupils to teach another pupil in the class about what they know about a topic or subject;
- encouraging pupils to 'pole bridge', where one pupil articulates what they are doing to embed learning to the class, or to another peer in a 'talking partner' pair;
- prompting pupils to use graphic representations to recall and organise prior and current knowledge (e.g. mind maps, flow charts, topic webs);
- using open questioning to probe and deepen pupils' learning;
- giving pupils a break between learning tasks and activities;
- encouraging pupils to self-evaluate at every stage in the learning process.

The Sutton Trust–EEF research undertaken in 2014 found that the impact of meta-cognition and self-regulation on learners added between seven to nine months' additional progress (Higgins *et al.* 2014). Similarly, pupils who demonstrate a wide range of meta-cognitive skills tend to perform better in external exams and complete work more efficiently.

Pupils who are good readers readily learn to use cognitive and meta-cognitive strategies effectively in order to develop a deeper understanding of a topic or subject area.

Those pupils with SEND who find reading difficult (e.g. those with an SpLD such as dyslexia) find it more difficult to acquire meta-cognitive skills, and therefore need teachers and their peers to explicitly model, teach and practise these skills with them regularly.

Teaching meta-cognitive strategies tends to be particularly effective with lower-attaining pupils with SEND. For example, meta-cognition is more effective in small groups, where pupils can support each other, and make their thinking explicit through discussion ('talking partners'). As pupils become more skilled at using meta-cognitive strategies, they gain more self-confidence to become independent learners.

Supporting pupils with SEND to become independent learners

The Department for Children, Schools and Families (DCSF) commissioned research on independent learning, with the report *Independent Learning: Literature Review* being published in 2008 (Meyer *et al.* 2008). This report clarified the concept of independent learning and the skills pupils need to develop this approach to learning; it identified the key elements of independent learning and the factors that influence successful independent learning; it confirmed the benefits of teachers promoting pupils' independent learning, particularly among those with SEND; and, it recommended a number of strategies teachers can use in enabling pupils to become independent learners.

To save busy trainee and qualified teachers time in reading the full DCSF report, the following section provides a summary of the key findings.

The concept of independent learning

Independent learning is frequently linked to other approaches such as pupil-centred learning, personalisation and pupil ownership of learning. However, the most common term used is 'self-regulated learning'. The DCSF report states: 'Supporting students in self-regulation, providing feedback and helping them highlight progress was found to be especially important among remedial readers and other students with special educational needs' (Meyer *et al.* 2008: 2).

Key factors enabling independent learning to occur

A number of external and internal factors influence successful independent learning. The external factors include:

- a strong teacher–pupil relationship based on trust;
- greater flexibility in the time that teachers give pupils to work on specific tasks;
- the establishment of an enabling environment (i.e. an appropriate physical environment conducive to learning, which includes access to information and communication technology (ICT)).

The internal factors include:

- pupils developing cognitive skills, focusing on memory, attention and problem solving;
- pupils developing meta-cognitive skills, associated with an understanding of how learning occurs (i.e. being able to listen, remember, apply knowledge previously

learnt, reflect on their learning, and monitor and self-assess their own learning and progress);

- pupils developing affective skills related to feelings and emotions (i.e. motivation, the ability to wait for achievement outcomes).

The benefits of independent learning for pupils with SEND

Independent learning has a number of benefits for pupils, including those with SEND. It:

- increases and improves self-motivation and confidence;
- improves academic performance;
- develops greater pupil self-awareness and understanding of their own learning effectiveness;
- improves pupils' management of their own learning;
- enables teachers to provide a wider variety of differentiated tasks and activities, tailored more readily to matching pupils' learning needs, and structuring group work.

How teachers can help to promote independent learning among pupils with SEND

The DCSF research on independent learning found a number of effective strategies teachers can employ to help to support pupils to become independent learners. These include:

- providing scaffolding to aid learning (e.g. using mind maps, writing frames, paired working with a proficient independent peer learner), all designed to enable pupils with SEND to eventually take greater ownership for developing their own ideas, and to solve problems;
- providing pupils with the opportunity to self-monitor (e.g. encouraging pupils with SEND to peer review and self-review, via AfL, and to monitor their learning through the use of internal and external feedback, in order to see whether the strategies they used in learning were effective for achieving their learning goals);
- modelling independent learning as a 'coach' (e.g. demonstrating to pupils practical approaches on how to be an effective independent learner, as part of everyday high-quality teaching and learning, i.e. giving pupils a problem or question to solve and explore further on the curriculum topic, either independently or in a group);
- building activities into lessons that help pupils to acquire and use thinking skills;
- promoting pupil voice (e.g. talking about learning with pupils, enabling them to become more aware of the steps involved in learning, and to understand their own learning styles better);
- providing pupils with feedback on their homework (e.g. to help to develop pupils' confidence in working independently outside school, and to help them to become more reflective independent learners);
- promoting creativity and a diversity of learning responses (e.g. offering pupils with SEND the opportunity to present their work in different ways, including using multi-media, written and oral presentations).

Class and subject teachers can find out more on independent learning from the evidence-based DCSF report (Meyer *et al.* 2008).

Setting relevant homework to enhance SEND pupils' learning and progress

The concept of homework

According to the EEF, homework refers to tasks given to pupils by their teachers to be completed outside of usual lessons. Common homework activities may include reading or preparing for work to be done in class, or practising or completing tasks or activities already taught or started in lessons. Homework may also include more extended activities to develop inquiry skills or more directed and focused work such as revision for tests and examinations. Pupils with SEND benefit greatly from homework tasks that are practical (e.g. using the computer to find out information, designing or making something, solving a real problem, preparing a presentation, or playing games that reinforce basic literacy and maths skills).

Homework is one of the main ways in which pupils can acquire the skill of independent learning. It also helps to reinforce, consolidate and extend learning done in school. Pupils with SEND get more out of a homework activity if their parents or carers get involved.

The Sutton Trust–EEF research into the impact that homework has on the attainment of pupils in primary and secondary schools revealed that homework is much less effective for primary-aged pupils, leading to less increase in learning, and more valuable and effective at secondary-school level, when it is used as a short and focused intervention, leading to an average of between five to eight months' additional progress (The Sutton Trust–EEF 2012; Higgins *et al.* 2014).

Top tips on setting homework for pupils with SEND

Class and subject teachers will find it useful to consult with the SENCO on what constitutes effective homework tasks for pupils with a diversity of SEND. Pupils with SEND who struggle with classwork in lessons may also find homework a challenge, particularly when they struggle with working memory and organisational skills. For some pupils with SEND, homework can become another negative experience, as they struggle to remember what they did in the lesson, and what the teacher said about how to go about completing the task set at home.

Listed below are the top ten tips teachers can use to make homework more accessible to pupils with SEND:

1 Give opportunities for pupils to pre-learn and over-learn key words and subject-specific terminology that they will meet in the homework.

2 Offer pre-tutoring and subject-specific definitions relevant to the homework topic.

3 Base homework tasks on the interests of pupils as well as the lesson topic.

4 Provide parents and carers with useful strategies to help them to support their child's learning at home (e.g. homework guidance booklet, DVDs/CDs or video clips that model homework support approaches, parent workshops on homework).

5 Reframe homework tasks to make them more appealing, interesting, fun and practical, and less reliant on written outcomes.

6 Give a concise time guideline, in relation to how long pupils with SEND should ideally spend completing the homework task.

7 Offer pupils with SEND the opportunity to succeed in completing the homework activity, while providing an appropriate level of challenge.

8 Set homework tasks that help to develop pupils' social skills, as well as their academic skills.

9 Set homework that is age appropriate to the phase of education (e.g. if a pupil with SEND has a reading age of ten and they are aged fourteen, the homework should be relevant and appeal to secondary-age teenage interests).

10 Seek advice from the SENCO on how to ensure that homework tasks using curriculum subject text match the reading age of pupils with SEND.

How to calculate the reading age of a text using the Gunning Fog Index

1 Select a typical example of subject text of about 100 words.

2 Count the number of words in the text extract.

3 Divide the number of words by the number of sentences to give the average sentence length.

4 Count the number of long words (i.e. those words with more than three syllables, excluding proper nouns, compound words, common suffixes like '-es', '-ed', '-ing').

5 Add the average sentence length to the number of long words.

6 Multiply the result by 0.4 to give you the Gunning Fog Index score, which will give the reading age comparison.

Teachers can also do this activity using the Gunning Fog Index online calculator (available at http://gunning-fog-index.com) by copying and pasting the subject text into the text box provided on the webpage and then clicking on the 'Calculate' button, which will give the reading age.

Further information about setting homework for pupils with SEND can be found at bit.ly/HomeworkStrategies and bit.ly/HomeworkCards, which offer useful advice for teachers relating to supporting pupils with autism to cope with homework.

An excellent video clip on the topic of homework can also be found at www.familylives.org.uk/advice/secondary/learning-school/homework, which offers parents and carers some practical tips on supporting their child with homework.

Questions for reflection

1 A pupil with SEND whom you teach has made less than expected progress. What action will you take to explore the reasons for this outcome, and how will you address future improvement in their progress over time?

continued

2 A pupil with dyslexia is really struggling to remember facts and key information related to a subject topic. What strategies will you employ to enable the pupil concerned to improve their memory skills?

3 How are you enabling pupils with SEND to develop meta-cognitive skills and strategies, in order to improve their learning and progress?

4 You have concerns about a pupil with SEND who is finding it difficult to become a confident independent learner. Describe the steps you will take to address this issue.

5 The parents of a pupil with SEND whom you teach inform you that getting their child to do their homework is a constant battle. What action will you take to enable homework for the pupil and their parents to become a more productive experience?

CHAPTER 3

Adapting teaching to respond to the strengths and needs of pupils with SEND

This chapter covers:

- Barriers to learning for pupils with SEND and how to overcome them
- Learning styles
- Differentiation to ensure effective teaching for pupils with SEND
- The features of high-quality teaching
- Using questioning
- Developing thinking skills
- Meeting the needs of pupils with high-incidence SEND
- Different stages of child development informing the adaptation of teaching

Barriers to learning for pupils with SEND and how to overcome them

When identifying barriers to learning, teachers and trainee teachers need to focus on the holistic needs of pupils with SEND as learners (i.e. the cognitive, educational, environmental, social and emotional factors that may be causing their barriers to learning). These may include any of the following:

- an unsuitable learning environment;
- inappropriate pupil groupings;
- ineffective deployment of TAs;
- a limited range of, and inflexible, teaching styles;
- inaccessible curriculum materials;
- no alternative forms of recording ideas or responses to tasks offered, other than in writing;
- inflexible timetabling;

- inappropriate curriculum and training options;

- poor teacher–pupil and/or poor TA–pupil relationships;

- poor literacy and numeracy skills;

- within-child barriers (e.g. unidentified emotional and mental health needs);

- unstable or difficult family/home circumstances;

- poor attendance at school.

Overcoming barriers to learning

The most popular and common approaches used to remove barriers to learning include the following:

- breaking tasks down into smaller, more manageable steps, to ensure that pupils with SEND achieve some early success in the learning process;

- curriculum and lesson planning that takes into account knowledge of the nature of pupils' SEND, how this may affect their access to learning, how they learn best, and their strengths and talents;

- using differentiation to make the curriculum accessible, with curriculum text matched to pupils' reading age;

- using the SEND pupils' preferred learning style, to enable them to grasp and understand more difficult concepts;

- using a range of different learning and teaching styles that will cater for VAK and tactile learners (multi-sensory learning).

Figure 3.1 offers teachers and trainee teachers a useful checklist with further suggestions for overcoming and removing barriers to learning and participation for pupils with SEND.

Learning styles

Pupils with SEND, like all pupils, employ different approaches or styles of learning. They are unlikely to use just one single style of learning. However, where they have difficulty grasping a concept in a subject area, they do benefit from the teacher explaining this concept using their preferred learning style.

Table 3.1 illustrates the four most popular learning and teaching styles.

The Sutton Trust–EEF research found that the teacher's chosen learning style had a low impact – in an average class of 25 pupils, only one or two actually benefited from the chosen approach (The Sutton Trust–EEF 2012; Higgins *et al.* 2014). The implications of this finding for teachers and trainee teachers are that learning styles need to be complemented by other teaching and learning approaches and strategies in order to remove barriers to learning.

Strategy	YES	NO
Teacher and TA have jointly pre-planned to ensure maximum curriculum access	❏	❏
Pupils with SEND are seated at the front of the class to ensure access and full participation	❏	❏
Appropriate differentiated learning objectives have been identified for pupils with SEND	❏	❏
Visual timetables are used which make the school day structure clearer	❏	❏
New subject-specific vocabulary is displayed, revisited and clarified with SEND pupils	❏	❏
SEND pupils explain back the teacher's instructions in their own words confirming understanding	❏	❏
Support is in place for pupils who have difficulty remembering information	❏	❏
Multi-sensory teaching approaches are used (e.g. VAK)	❏	❏
Pupils are given a role by the teacher that ensures they are active participants in the lesson	❏	❏
Real artefacts, concrete apparatus, symbols and photographs are used	❏	❏
Pre-tutoring is used with SEND pupils to improve their access to learning	❏	❏
Peer buddies provide positive role models as learners, for pupils with SEND	❏	❏
Pupils with SEND benefit from 'talking partner' work with another peer, to share their ideas and thinking	❏	❏
Differentiated thinking time to answer questions is given to pupils (e.g. three seconds for a closed-question response and ten seconds for an open-question response)	❏	❏
A mixture of open and closed questions are used in a 50:50 ratio by the teacher	❏	❏
A distraction-free quiet learning area is provided in the classroom for those with ASD	❏	❏
Classroom rules are available in different formats (e.g. visual)	❏	❏
A variety of pupil groupings are used to promote collaborative learning	❏	❏
The teacher models tasks and activities, which are accompanied by clear explanations	❏	❏
Scaffolding is used to support pupils' learning (e.g. writing frames, mind maps, prompt cards)	❏	❏
Alternatives to written recording are available to pupils with SEND	❏	❏
Effective use is made of multi-media technology and augmentive communication technology	❏	❏
Links are made in learning to pupils' own experiences and current understanding	❏	❏
Learning from additional interventions is transferred across the curriculum, via cross-curricular links	❏	❏
Pupils are given positive, sensitive and constructive feedback if they misunderstand a concept or give an incorrect answer	❏	❏
Rewards and sanctions are used appropriately for behaviour	❏	❏
Curriculum materials reflect diversity (e.g. ethnicity, disability, gender)	❏	❏
Tasks, activities and new learning are broken down into smaller steps or chunks for SEND pupils	❏	❏

Figure 3.1 Checklist for removing barriers to learning and participation

Table 3.1

Learning and teaching styles

AUDITORY

Characteristics:
Good listener; fluent, expressive talker; good vocabulary; explains things clearly to others; enjoys brainstorming; quick to learn from listening to others; self-talks; thinks aloud; sequences and organises information.

Learns least when:
Unclear guidance on how to do a task is given, lengthy descriptions are given, or information is repeated.

Appropriate teaching approaches:
Use audio activities; provide opportunities to discuss in groups; give opportunity for oral feedback; use investigative reporting and interviewing; give opportunities for pupils to express ideas in their own words.

LOGICAL/THEORIST

Characteristics:
Enjoys knowing and applying theories, concepts, models and principles; likes logical explanations; enjoys estimating, problem solving and doing quizzes and puzzles; works through tasks in an orderly and methodical way; can identify connecting links.

Learns least when:
Feelings or emotions are involved, tasks are ambiguous and unstructured, or they are 'put on the spot'.

Appropriate teaching approaches:
Provide step-by-step plans and instructions; use data in a variety of forms; provide a theory or principle to work from; give them time to explore ideas and think things through.

VISUAL

Characteristics:
Observant; quick to see things others miss; photographic memory; good sense of direction; good imagination; good at visualising events and information; needs to watch and think things through; responds best to visual approaches.

Learns least when:
Under time constraints, they cannot see any relevance in the task, or they do not spend enough time or pay enough attention to specific detail.

Appropriate teaching approaches:
Use visual materials, videos, websites and digital technology; introduce flow charts and diagrams, mind maps and brainstorming; use picture sequencing and visualisation exercises; highlighting text, drawing to demonstrate their understanding of a text.

KINAESTHETIC/ACTIVIST

Characteristics:
Enjoys teamwork and doing practical activities; has good coordination and manual dexterity; enjoys concrete experiences; learns by example, demonstration and modelling; remembers by doing; fidgets; easily distracted; impulsive.

Learns least when:
Passive, work is solitary, they are asked to attend to theory or detail, or oral or written information is given.

Appropriate teaching approaches:
Provide opportunities to touch and manipulate objects, build models and participate in activity-based learning; investigation and experimental work.

© 2015, *Special Educational Needs for Qualified and Trainee Teachers*, Rita Cheminais, Routledge.

I learn best by:

☐ Seeing and looking (Visual)

☐ hearing and listening (Auditory)

☐ making and doing (Kinaesthetic)

☐ VAK — using all three learning styles

Which ONE learning style helps you learn best?

_____

Maple School

My Learning Log

This learning log belongs to:

_____

Class/Form: _____

I like to learn in lessons best by being

☐ On my own ☐ With a friend

☐ In a group ☐ With the whole class

(You can tick ✓ more than one box above)

What aids to learning do you like to use?

☐ PC/Tablet ☐ TV/DVD/YouTube

☐ iPod/Radio ☐ Blog/Podcasts

☐ Encyclopaedia/Dictionary/Thesaurus

☐ Wikipedia/Internet/Grammar and Spellchecker

(You can tick ✓ more than one box above)

The other places I like to learn outside school are

☐ Home ☐ Local library

☐ Friend's house ☐ Grandparents' house

Other (please state where) _____

_____

I find learning easy when
_____

I find learning hard when
_____

The things that stop me learning in lessons are
_____

I enjoy learning most when
_____

The things that would help me to learn better are
_____

I remember things for a test or lesson by
_____

Who helps me learn?

Teachers ☐ Parents/Carers ☐

Teaching assistant ☐ Brothers/Sisters ☐

Learning mentor ☐ Aunts/Uncles ☐

Friends ☐ Grandparents ☐

Study buddy ☐ Neighbours ☐

(You can tick ✔ more than one box above)

I know when I've learned something well because

_____

I talk about my learning most with

_____

The person/people who have taught me how to learn is/are

_____

The most important thing I've learnt this year is

_____

The most interesting thing I've learnt this year is

_____

The least interesting thing I've learnt this year is

_____

I find learning boring when

_____

I find homework helps me to learn when it

_____

If I find learning/homework hard, I get help from

_____

My learning targets for the term are

1.

2.

3.

The one colour that shows how I feel about my learning is

GREEN = I understand fully what I am taught

AMBER = I sometimes understand what I'm taught

RED = I don't understand a lot of what I'm taught

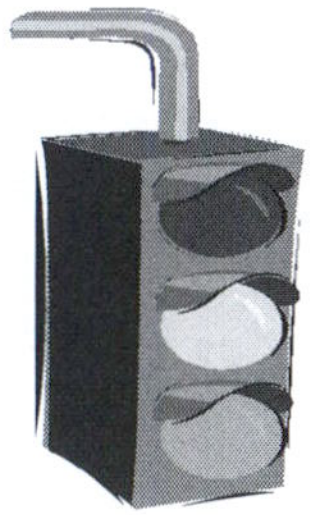

To help me achieve these targets, I need

1.

2.

3.

The one other thing I wish to tell my class or form teacher about my learning is

Figure 3.2 Model pupil learning log

© 2015, *Special Educational Needs for Qualified and Trainee Teachers*, Rita Cheminais, Routledge.

Differentiation to ensure effective teaching for pupils with SEND

The concept of differentiation

Differentiation is defined as the process by which curriculum objectives, teaching methods, assessment, resources and learning activities are planned and adjusted to cater for, and match the needs of, pupils with SEND. In other words, differentiation is the process by which differences between learners are accommodated, to enable all pupils in a group to have the best chance of learning. It is anything a teacher does that helps to personalise learning.

Teacher planning reflects differentiation in its simplest form, when it indicates:

- **must** – all learners can grasp the key concepts and meet the lesson objectives;
- **should** – most learners (average ability) can complete work set;
- **could** – some learners (higher ability) can also complete extension tasks.

Why differentiate?

Differentiation ensures equality of learning opportunities to enable all learners, irrespective of their ability, to make progress. It offers a range of strategies, activities and techniques that allow teachers to secure the best progress possible for the pupils in their classes.

Approaches to differentiation

There are seven popular approaches to differentiation:

1 **Task:** Differentiation by task involves the teacher setting and producing different tasks and exercises, on the same curriculum topic or theme, to match pupils' differing abilities. The teacher can alternatively use the same single worksheet with all pupils, which is comprised of graduated tasks that get progressively harder. Lower-ability pupils with SEND would do some of the early tasks set, while higher-ability pupils would be expected to complete all tasks set.

2 **Grouping:** Pupils with SEND can work in a variety of different grouping arrangements (e.g. in a mixed ability group, a gender group, a friendship group or an ability group) to undertake a task set by the teacher. The grouping arrangement enables pupils with SEND to benefit from peer support and peer modelling of good learning. Each pupil in the group is allocated a different role by the teacher, and the group work together collaboratively in order to complete the given task. For example, each group is asked to prepare some writing to persuade an audience to use or buy a particular product. Pupils can present their end product as a team in different ways (e.g. as a poster, a leaflet, a YouTube video clip).

3 **Resources:** The teacher offers advanced resources and multiple materials that help to approach the given topic from different angles. For example, some pupils with SEND may require simpler text matched to their reading age with illustrations, while higher-ability pupils work with more advanced materials and complex text. Resources and materials for learning include digital and multi-media technology.

4 Pace: The teacher sets deadlines for task completion in the lesson, which vary according to pupils' abilities and the nature of their SEND.

5 Outcome: This is where all pupils undertake the same given task, but a variety of results are expected and accepted by the teacher. Pupils tackle the task at their own level and produce outcomes that reflect their understanding of the task, and their ability to carry it out. This is not always an ideal approach to use with pupils with SEND, who value a more structured approach.

6 Response (Dialogue and Support): This is the question-and-answer approach where the teacher facilitates problem solving by asking pupils questions and explaining in language tailored to the abilities of the pupils. A mixture of open and closed questioning is used, with thinking time extended to improve pupils' responses. Pupils with SEND are given verbal support and encouragement to ensure that they can participate with more confidence and can ask the teacher questions.

7 Assessment: This is ongoing assessment of pupils' learning by the teacher throughout the lesson, which enables other methods of differentiation to be adjusted, according to the pupils' needs as learners.

Good practice in a differentiated classroom

The following good practice would be observed in a classroom with effective differentiation:

- Learning experiences are based on a diagnosis of pupils' readiness for learning, their interest and their learning needs.
- Content, activities, resources and assessments are developed in response to the differing needs of a diversity of learners.
- Teaching and learning are focused on key concepts, understanding and skill acquisition.
- All pupils are participating in appropriate learning.
- The teacher and pupils work together to ensure that continual engagement and a sufficient level of challenge is present in learning.
- The teacher effectively coordinates the use of lesson time, learning space and the activities set.
- Flexible learning arrangements exist (e.g. independent work, paired work, group work, whole-class learning).
- AfL takes place, which enables pupils to reflect upon and self-review their own learning.

Key questions for teachers on differentiation for pupils with SEND

- Are lesson objectives providing an appropriate challenge for pupils with SEND?
- Does the work set build on pupils' prior attainment?
- Does the work set allow pupils with SEND to succeed at their own level?
- Are activities well planned to remove any barriers to participation?
- Do the tasks set offer the most effective way for pupils with SEND to achieve the expected outcomes?

- Do the activities set accommodate SEND pupils' attention span and pace of work?
- Can the pupils with SEND work without continual reassurance from the teacher?
- Do the learning outcomes of pupils with SEND inform the planning of future work for them?

The features of high-quality teaching

High-quality teaching is that which is differentiated and personalised to meet the needs of the majority of pupils, including those with SEND. Previously referred to as 'quality first teaching', it is part of the daily repertoire of teaching strategies that ensures SEND pupils' progression in learning. The draft 2014 *SEND Code of Practice* comments:

> High quality teaching, differentiated for individual pupils, is the first step in responding to pupils who have or may have SEN. . . . Schools should regularly and carefully review the quality of teaching for all pupils including those at risk of underachievement. This includes reviewing and, where necessary, improving teachers' understanding of strategies to identify and support vulnerable pupils and their knowledge of the SEN most frequently encountered.
>
> (DfE 2014g: 6.34)

The following features of high-quality teaching would be observed in classrooms:

- Lessons are differentiated and personalised to match learners' needs, and in particular curriculum resources used are matched to SEND pupils' reading age (Ofsted will track this across the curriculum for pupils with SEND).
- Pupils as active participants are cooperative learners in the learning process.
- Learning builds on prior knowledge and understanding.
- Links are made to the transfer of learning across the curriculum.
- Teachers use a range of teaching approaches (VAK).
- Pupil voice is encouraged, with AfL embedded.
- Pupils accept responsibility for their own learning, and are given the opportunity to work independently.
- Pupils are given the opportunity in the lesson to review their learning (e.g. 'Three new things I have learned in today's lesson are . . .').
- Pupils develop confidence and persistence in learning (e.g. pupil mistakes are turned into positive learning opportunities – peer coaching is used).
- ICT, digital and multi-media technology is used and applied to enhance curriculum access, extend learning and demonstrate understanding.
- Teachers and TAs make regular use of encouragement and authentic praise to engage and motivate pupils with SEND.
- Pupils talk about their learning, and think aloud (e.g. tell other pupils how they found an answer or solved the given problem).
- Teachers and TAs model good learning, explanation, the use of open questioning, thinking aloud and mind mapping.
- Meta-cognition is evident (i.e. pupils know how to learn, they think about thinking, they problem solve, they question, and they do this together with other peers, as collaborative learners).

Using questioning

Questioning accounts for up to one-third of all teaching and learning time, with teachers on average asking a class of pupils up to two questions every minute. The quality and type of questions asked is more important than the number of questions learners are asked in any lesson by teachers. A good-quality open question poses a challenge that helps to extend pupils' thinking.

The use of questioning is a key means of transferring knowledge, and leads to more effective learning. Questioning helps to motivate pupils, assess their learning and promote reflection, analysis and enquiry.

The purpose of questioning

The purpose of using questioning when teaching pupils with SEND is to:

- ensure that pupils are active, interested, alert, engaged and challenged participants in the learning process;
- help to reveal any misunderstandings or misconceptions and to turn these into positive learning opportunities;
- enable pupils to reflect on given information and to remember it;
- help pupils to develop their thinking skills;
- promote reasoning, problem solving, evaluation and the formulation of hypotheses that are cross-curricular thinking skills;
- focus pupils' thinking on key concepts and issues;
- encourage pupils to discuss ideas;
- extend pupils' thinking from the concrete and factual to the analytical and evaluative;
- enable teachers to check pupils' prior knowledge and their understanding;
- enable pupils to mobilise and recall existing knowledge and experiences to create new understanding and meaning;
- promote pupils' thinking about the way they have learned.

Types of questions

Initially, there are two basic types of questions:

1 **closed** lower-order factual recall questions – these require pupils to remember, and have a single right answer, and help to check knowledge and understanding (e.g. 'What?', 'Who?', 'When?', 'Where?');

2 **open** higher-order thought-provoking questions – these require pupils to think, and have a range of possible responses (e.g. 'How?', 'Why?').

Practical strategies for teachers using questioning

As part of high-quality teaching, teachers should:

- ensure that they use a combination of higher-order and lower-order questions in proportion of 50 per cent for each;

- dependent on the ability range of pupils with SEND, model how to ask and answer questions;

- use an appropriate waiting time to elicit pupils' responses to questions posed (e.g. wait at least three seconds for the response to a lower-order closed question, and ten seconds for the response to a higher-order open question);

- consider extending the waiting time beyond ten seconds to enable the pupil to revise and expand upon their response, and to encourage other pupils to contribute;

- wherever the opportunity arises, pose a higher-order open question at the end of a lesson to stimulate pupils' thinking in readiness for discussion the next day;

- keep pupils with SEND on task by asking quick-fire lower-order closed questions;

- ask questions that require a collective group response, rather than an individual pupil response, where the teacher knows that pupils with SEND may find answering questions a stressful process, for fear of giving the incorrect answer;

- tailor questions to match the abilities of the pupils (e.g. differentiate the response level by giving less able pupils learning resources or curriculum materials to refer to for finding the answer, whereas with more able pupils pose the question first without providing them with any curriculum materials to refer to);

- ask pupils questions sequentially by starting off with lower-order questions and building up to higher-order questions;

- ensure that the learning environment is emotionally intelligent with a 'no-blame' culture, where it is OK to give an incorrect response to a question.

Teacher strategies for encouraging pupils to ask questions

- Offer pupils with SEND the opportunity to pose a range of questions related to the topic that they would like answered in future lessons.

- Ask pupils with SEND to set questions at the end of a topic for other pupils in the group or class to answer, awarding praise or marks for the quality of the question posed rather than for the answer.

- Provide opportunities during lessons to enable pupils with SEND to use an internet search engine to pose enquiries, working in a small group or in pairs, or individually.

- Create a question wall area in the classroom, where pupils and the teacher can post questions they would like to find the answer to, related to the topic.

- To enable more reticent pupils with SEND to participate and be included in asking questions, use a question box with Post-it notes.

- Ask pupils with SEND to bring a question related to the topic or concept being taught to the next lesson.

- Consider having one or two key questions written down for the pupils with SEND and structure the learning around exploring the answers to these questions.

- With more confident pupils with SEND, use hot seating, where pupils take turns to be a character from history, literature or current affairs, and other pupils ask them questions related to the context.

Questions that help pupils with SEND to assess their own learning

Listed below are some basic questions teachers may find helpful to use to support pupils with SEND self-reviewing their own learning and progress:

- What have I learned?
- What have I found difficult?
- What do I need to learn next?
- What would help me to do better?

Developing thinking skills

Thinking skills, as part of high-quality teaching, are a series of cross-curricular lower-order and higher-order thinking skills that enable pupils to understand the process of meaningful learning: how to think flexibly, and how to make reasoned judgements. They entail pupils processing information, reasoning, enquiring, evaluating and thinking creatively.

Table 3.2 offers teachers a range of suggested questions to support pupils' higher-order thinking skills, in lessons across the curriculum.

Table 3.3 provides teachers with an at-a-glance guide to Benjamin Bloom's taxonomy of thinking skills. Teachers and trainee teachers may find the activities and questions for each thinking skill a useful prompt for informing the planning of appropriate activities.

Knowledge, Comprehension and Application are the lower-order thinking skills, while Analysis, Synthesis and Evaluation are the higher-order thinking skills. Generally, pupils with SEND are able to master the lower-order thinking skills, with support.

An understanding of SEND pupils' needs as learners is central to high-quality teaching, as it informs the range of strategies that teachers consider using, the nature of the provision and the nature of reasonable adjustments to be made.

Meeting the needs of pupils with high-incidence SEND

High-incidence SEND fit into four broad areas:

1 communication and interaction;
2 cognition and learning;
3 social, emotional and mental health;
4 sensory and/or physical needs.

The draft 2014 *SEND Code of Practice* comments: 'In practice, individual children or young people often have needs that cut across all these areas and their needs may change over time' (DfE 2014g: 6.24).

High-quality personalised teaching, differentiated for individual pupils, is the first step in responding to pupils who have been identified as having SEND. The draft 2014 *SEND Code of Practice* comments:

> Early years providers, schools and colleges should know precisely where children and young people are in their learning and development. They should:

Table 3.2

Questioning to support pupils' higher-order thinking skills

Applying knowledge	Analysing understanding	Synthesising thinking	Evaluating
Can you explain why/how/which . . .?	How would you group, sort, categorise or classify . . .?	Can you think of a better way to . . .?	How successful was . . .?
What would you have done . . .?	Can you work out the parts, features or structure of . . .?	What would you have done if . . .?	How would you rate . . .?
What do you think will happen/would have happened next . . .?	How can you show the differences and similarities of . . .?	How would you tackle this next time?	What do you think of . . .?
What makes you think . . .?	What patterns can you find?	How would you change/adapt to make a new . . .?	What makes . . . good/bad/average?
What would you use for . . .?	What evidence can you find to . . .?	Given the choice, what would you do . . .?	

(Source: Smith 2007: 10)

Table 3.3

Bloom's taxonomy of thinking skills

Thinking skill objective	Definition with link to thinking	What pupils need to do		Examples of question prompts
6. Evaluation	The ability to judge the value of something using criteria to support the judgement. Evaluation questions expect pupils to use their knowledge to form judgements, and defend the positions or viewpoints they take up. Evaluation demands very complex thinking and reasoning.	Appraise Argue Assess Critique Defend Evaluate Give opinion/viewpoint Grade Judge Justify Rate Recommend	Select	What do you think about . . .? What are your criteria for assessing . . .? Which is more important/moral/logical? What inconsistencies are there in . . .? What errors are there? Why is the . . . valid? How can you defend . . .? Why is the order important? Why does it change? Why is it better?
5. Synthesis	The ability to re-form individual parts to make a new whole. Synthesis questions demand that pupils combine and select from available knowledge to respond to unfamiliar situations or solve new problems.	Arrange Be original Combine Compose Construct Create Design Forecast Formulate Hypothesise	Imagine Invent Organise Re- organise	What could we add to improve/design/solve . . .? Propose an alternative . . . What conclusion can you draw? How else would you . . .? State a rule. How do the writers differ in their response to . . .? What happens at the beginning of the story poem and how does it change?
4. Analysis	The ability to understand how parts relate to a whole, and understand structure and motive. Analysis questions require pupils to break down what they know and reassemble it to help them to solve a problem.	Analyse Break down Categorise Classify Compare and contrast Criticise Differentiate Discern fact from opinion Explore Infer Investigate	Question Relate Support Test	What is the evidence for parts or features of . . . .? Separate fact from opinion. What is the function or purpose of . . .? What assumptions are being made and why? What is the evidence? State the point of view. Make a distinction between . . . and . . . What is this really saying? What does this symbolise?

Thinking skill objective	Definition with link to thinking	What pupils need to do	Examples of question prompts
3. Application	The ability to transfer knowledge learned in one situation or context to another. Questions in this aspect require pupils to use their existing knowledge and understanding to solve a new problem or to make sense of a new context.	Apply to a new context Demonstrate Employ Interpret Model Predict Show how Solve Use	What other examples are there? What shape of graph are you expecting? What do you think will happen and why? Where else might this be useful? How can you use a spreadsheet to . . .? Can you apply what you now know to solve . . .? What does this suggest to you? How does the writer do this? What would the next line of my modelled answer be? How can you best demonstrate your understanding? If you did this again, what would you do differently?
2. Comprehension	The ability to demonstrate basic understanding of concepts and the curriculum, and translate this into other words. Comprehension questions require pupils to process the knowledge they already have in order to answer the question.	Edit Extend Explain Give examples of Illustrate Report Restate Review Simplify Summarise Translate	What do we mean by . . .? Explain. How do you think . . .? Why do you think that . . .? What might this mean? Explain what a spreadsheet does. What are the key features of . . .? Explain your model. What is known about . . .? What happens when . . .? What word represents . . .? What is significant about . . .? Can you think of any other similarities? What do you consider essential . . .?

Table 3.3 (continued)

Bloom's taxonomy of thinking skills

Thinking skill objective	Definition with link to thinking	What pupils need to do	Examples of question prompts
1. Knowledge	The ability to remember something learned previously. Pupils will need to link aspects of knowledge necessary for a task to other relevant information.	Define Describe Find Identify Label List facts Locate Match Memorise Name Recall information Recite Remember Tell	Who, what, where, when, how? Describe what you see. What is the name for . . .? Which is the best one? Where in the book would you find . . .? What are the types of graph? What are we looking for in . . .? Where is this set? Which three things are the most important? List the key characters in the story.

- ensure that decisions are informed by the insights of parents and carers, and of children and young people themselves;
- have high ambitions and set stretching targets for them;
- track their progress towards these goals;
- keep under review the additional or different provision that is made for them;
- promote positive outcomes in the wider areas of personal and social development; and
- ensure that the approaches used are based on the best possible evidence and are having the required impact on progress.

(DfE 2014g: 1.25)

In their SEND review (2010), Ofsted identified that:

> The best learning occurred in all types of provision when teachers or other lead adults had a thorough and detailed knowledge of the children and young people; a thorough knowledge and understanding of teaching and learning strategies and techniques, as well as the subject areas of learning being taught; and a sound understanding of child development and how different learning difficulties and disabilities influence this.

(Ofsted 2010: 11)

Teachers and trainee teachers may find Table 3.4 a useful aide memoire to refer to, in relation to knowing how to meet the needs of pupils with SEND, who fall in to the four broad areas of SEND. Table 3.4 also includes meeting the needs of pupils with English as an additional language (EAL) and higher-ability pupils, some of whom may also have SEND.

The draft 2014 *SEND Code of Practice* recommends a graduated approach to meeting the needs of pupils with high-incidence SEND, which has been outlined in Table 1.1 of this book (p. 14) and explained in further detail in Chapter 2.

Different stages of child development informing the adaptation of teaching

The concept of child development and developmental milestones

Child development refers to the stepped progress children make in acquiring physical, social, emotional, cognitive (intellectual) and language skills during particular developmental time periods (e.g. aged 0–3, 3–7, 7–12 and 12–19), measured against expected levels of progression in each skill area, which are known as developmental milestones. Developmental milestones not only mark the achievement of certain abilities in the skill areas, but also signal the end of one developmental period and the beginning of another.

The areas of child development

All areas of child development are as important as each other and all impact on one another. Generally, children need to learn developmental skills in a consecutive order. Table 3.5 provides a general explanation of each developmental skill area, with general practical support strategies that can help to inform the adaptation of teaching.

Table 3.4

Meeting the needs of pupils with high-incidence SEND and additional educational needs

Communication and interaction

Which children: Speech, language and communication needs (SLCN), specific learning difficulties (SpLD), autistic spectrum disorders (ASD), specific learning hearing impaired (HI).

Barriers to learning:

– Difficulty with communication because they do not understand what others have said, or they cannot form sounds, words or sentences (SLCN) (HI).
– Difficulty in recognising words and difficulty with fine motor skills (writing) and coordination (SpLD).
– Difficulty with comprehending/understanding some communication and instructions (masked by learned phrases or echoing what the teacher says) (ASD).
– Difficulty with social interaction and imagination (ASD).
– Easily distracted, cannot cope with any change in routine and gets upset by certain stimuli (e.g. loud noise) (ASD).

Strategies to meet needs:

– Use shorter sentences.
– Speak clearly and avoid speaking too quickly.
– Pair the pupil up with another peer who is a good language role model, and with a supportive group of friends.
– Give the pupil simple messages to take to other peers or staff (verbal and written).
– Use open questioning, giving the pupil time to respond.
– Read aloud and use commentary to improve the pupil's listening skills.
– Use discussion and visual cues (e.g. symbols, pictures, photographs) to support written communication.
– Use props to encourage the pupil to talk more (e.g. telephone, audio recorders, digital camera, digital video camera, iPad).
– Engage the pupil in sequencing and matching activities to develop language.
– Teach language skills through games (e.g. 20 questions, role play, guessing games using verbal cues, hot seating).

Cognition and learning

Which children: Moderate learning difficulties (MLD), severe learning difficulties (SLD), profound and multiple learning difficulties (PMLD), specific learning difficulties (SpLD).

Barriers to learning:

– Difficulties with reading, writing, spelling and numbers; poor coordination; poor concentration and lack of spatial awareness; mismatch between achievement and ability; poor behaviour as a result of being a frustrated learner (SpLD).
– Learns at a slower pace; difficulty acquiring basic skills in literacy and numeracy; difficulty understanding concepts; low self-esteem; some language delay; poor concentration; underdeveloped social skills (MLD, SLD).
– Poor self-help skills; poor coordination and perception; severe and multiple learning difficulties with physical or sensory impairment (PMLD).

Strategies to meet needs:

– Give extra time where needed, allowing the pupil to work at their own pace.
– Break learning and tasks down into smaller steps.
– Give step-by-step instructions and write down homework for them.
– Model what you want the pupil to do (demonstration).
– Provide breaks between learning tasks.
– Support written tasks with mind maps, writing frames, prompt cards, word lists, visual prompts and symbols.
– Check the pupil's understanding by asking them to repeat back what you have said and asked them to do, and to say what they have learned in the lesson.
– Allow the pupil to present their work/responses in a range of ways other than writing (e.g. using multi-media, ICT).
– Use a range of multi-sensory teaching and learning approaches (VAK).
– Give immediate positive praise and feedback to reward effort/outcomes.
– Provide opportunities for overlearning to consolidate, and use peer-to-peer tutoring.
– Give the pupil sufficient thinking time to process information.

- Provide a quiet area for talking and listening activities in the classroom.
- Provide key vocabulary and word lists.
- Pre-tutor the pupil before lesson to familiarise them with new vocabulary.

Social, emotional and mental health difficulties

Which children: Attention deficit disorder (ADD), attention deficit hyperactivity disorder (ADHD), obsessive compulsive disorder (OCD), oppositional defiance disorder (ODD), autistic spectrum disorder (ASD), including Asperger's syndrome and autism, bipolar disorder, anxiety disorder.

Barriers to learning:

- Immature social skills, difficulty in making friends, withdrawn, socially isolated.
- Challenging, disruptive or disturbing behaviour; aggressive behaviour.
- Depression, mood swings.
- Self-harming, eating disorders, substance misuse.

Strategies to meet needs:

- Consistently apply classroom/school rules for behaviour.
- Model good behaviour for learning, and pair the pupil up with a positive peer role model.
- Incorporate turn-taking cooperative learning activities in lessons.
- Give one instruction and one task at a time; do not overwhelm the pupil.
- Catch the pupil being good, use positive praise and focus on the pupil's strengths, talents and interests.
- Defuse confrontation with humour, change the subject, send the pupil on a message or give them a classroom responsibility.
- Provide time out in a quiet, calm distraction-free area of the classroom.
- Provide them with anger management strategies (e.g. count to 10, deep breathing, use a stress ball, sit on hands).
- Seat the pupil at the front of the classroom away from busy areas and distractions (e.g. away from windows and doors).
- Use non-verbal cues to deal with minor behaviour (e.g. raised eyebrows, being silent, making eye contact, use symbols, i.e. thumbs up, thumbs down; traffic light colours for mood, understanding).

- Enable the pupil to work in pairs, in a small group, independently and in the whole class.

Sensory and/or physical needs

Which children: Visually impaired (VI), hearing impaired (HI), multi-sensory impaired (MSI), physical disability (PD).

Barriers to learning:

- Limited mobility, physical tiredness due to side effects of medication or medical condition, poor concentration (PD).
- Unable to distinguish or hear sounds and speech (HI).
- Unable to see fully or partially (VI).
- Unable to see, hear or speak (MSI).

Strategies to meet needs:

- Ensure the pupil can see the interactive whiteboard, TV or PC monitor (non VI).
- Use a visualiser or enlarged text, or put text onto an audio player (VI).
- Dim bright light to reduce glare, use window blinds or re-seat the pupil (VI).
- Provide a reader, where appropriate (VI).
- Produce written text in a range of alternative multi-media formats.
- Provide extra time for completing tasks and tests.
- Face the pupil when speaking so they can lip-read (HI).
- Use a hearing loop or lapel microphone (HI).
- Use subtitles on TV and video clips, and provide written transcripts (HI).
- Make use of visual or talking timetables and pre-tutoring (HI, VI).
- Ensure any misunderstandings, mistakes or misconceptions are dealt with sensitively and positively in the classroom.
- Give breaks between learning activities.
- Ensure safe movement around the classroom for wheelchair users (PD).
- Ensure learning resources for pupil use are accessible and clearly labelled (PD, VI).
- Seat the pupil at the front of the class, away from busy areas (e.g. doors and windows) to avoid distractions and background noise.
- Pair the pupil up with other peers and enable them to work in a supportive group of peers (VI, HI, MSI, PD).

Table 3.4 (continued)

Meeting the needs of pupils with high-incidence SEND and additional educational needs.

– Incorporate social stories in lessons, where appropriate, to help them understand feelings and develop empathy.
– Use role play, hot seating and drama activities.
– Develop their resilience: it is OK to make mistakes, adopt a fresh start and 'can-do' approach.
– Use visual timetables, symbols and pictorial instructions.
– Prepare the pupil in advance for any change in routines.
– Make teacher expectations clear.
– Provide access to multi-media technology for task completion.

English as an additional language (EAL)

Strategies to meet needs:

– Use plenty of visual clues and real objects.
– Ensure classroom displays use dual-language labelling.
– Use dual word banks and bilingual dictionaries.
– Provide collaborative activities that involve talking and role play with peers.
– Model key language features and structures by demonstration.
– Provide opportunities for the pupil to report back to other peers in the class.
– Place the pupil in supportive groups of peers with good readers and writers who can model English language skills.
– Provide opportunities for the pupil to use their first language, transferring their knowledge to English.
– Use the *A Language for All* EAL scale for assessing progress in English language skills.

Higher ability

Strategies to meet needs:

– Set open-ended tasks.
– Use open questioning.
– Provide plenty of opportunities to use multiple intelligences.
– Develop the pupil's higher-order thinking skills (e.g. analysis, synthesis, evaluation).
– Provide opportunities to develop their research skills (e.g. skimming, scanning, summarising, extracting facts from internet research).
– Use 'hot seating' and role play.
– Put an extra challenge on learning (e.g. word limits, time limits).
– Develop their analytical skills (e.g. investigative reporting).
– Set a quiz question, puzzle, problem or unusual word for the week.
– Give them a choice on how they present their work and findings.
– Seek opportunities for cross-phase and cross-Key Stage working.
– Provide emotional support, particularly if the pupil is being accelerated into groups with older peers.
– Give the pupil opportunities to work with external experts such as sports coaches or lecturers from university in their specialist area of high ability.

Table 3.5

Child development areas with recommended support strategies

Physical development	Cognitive development	Social and emotional development	Communication development
Movement skills, gross motor skills, fine motor skills, hand–eye coordination	Attention span, understanding information, reasoning, developing memory, logical thinking, questioning	Forming relationships, learning social skills, caring for others, self-reliance, making decisions, developing self-confidence, dealing with emotions	Understanding and acquiring language, developing vocabulary, body language (non-verbal communication)
Support strategies	**Support strategies**	**Support strategies**	**Support strategies**
– Provide space and some equipment for the development of movement skills and gross motor skills and adequate supervision. – Provide material and equipment for the improvement of fine motor skills (e.g. crayons, paint brushes, building blocks, puzzles). – Provide creative practical activities to enhance hand–eye coordination (e.g. cooking, art and craft activities). – Provide things to look at and varied visual experiences. – Provide an interesting environment.	– Develop the memory by talking about what has happened in the past. – Talk about what the pupil sees, hears, smells, touches and tastes. – Provide opportunities for touching real items (e.g. plants, animals). – Play 'I Spy' observational games. – Look at digital technology and machines. – Provide imaginative play (e.g. dressing up, having a shop). – Provide creative art/craft activities (e.g. painting). – Ask and answer questions and suggest ideas. – Give the pupil some individual time each day.	– Guide the child but respect their choices. – Let children meet and spend time with others. – Provide sharing and turn-taking activities. – Give support, praise, encouragement and supervision in the right amounts. – Provide the chance to share in decisions. – Listen to children and take them seriously. – Give children responsibility. – Emotional development: – Be warm and affectionate. – Let them express how they feel. – Make them feel secure and valued by reassurance. – Give them time and attention to adjust to new situations.	– Ask open-ended questions. – Discuss books, pictures, objects and sounds. – Ask children to recall something from the past. – Ask children to give information about themselves.

(Source: Home Learning College 2007: 5–16)

Table 3.6 provides a more in-depth guide to the developmental milestones that occur at particular ages during each developmental period. This will also help to inform the adaptation of teaching to address each one of the developmental skill areas for the relevant age group being taught.

Developmental delay

A developmental delay occurs if a child does not reach a milestone within a certain expected time period. Developmental delays can occur in one or more areas of development, or in all areas of development. As each area of development is related to growth in other areas, if a developmental delay arises in one area, it can have a 'knock-on' effect on other skills, thus putting a child at greater risk of having developmental delays in other areas of development.

Risk factors influencing development delay

The following risk factors can influence a child's development, and subsequent delay in development:

- **within-child factors** – e.g. health; personal characteristics; motivation and behaviour;

- **family and home circumstances** – e.g. poor relationships with parents, carers and/or siblings; a substandard home environment where there is a lack of basic amenities or space to learn and grow; a lack of emotional support and care in the family and home environment; no positive role models for the child in the family;

- **the community environment** – e.g. nowhere safe to play outside the home; a lack of local amenities; a poor environment as a result of socio-economic deprivation; 'ghetto' estates with a 'gang' culture; impoverished neighbourhoods; a lack of community spirit and sense of belonging;

- **learning background** – e.g. little (if any) exposure to regular formal education at play groups, nursery and school; little (if any) exposure to informal learning in the home environment, because the family may be in crisis or vulnerable, or because parents or carers have poor parenting skills.

Negative experiences for the child in one or more of the above circumstances can impair normal brain development, thus affecting the child's ability to acquire the basic core skills necessary for reaching the expected developmental milestones. This in turn results in the child requiring additional support with their learning and well-being. As the four risk factor contexts are inter-related, it makes it even more important for teachers to take a holistic approach when looking at how best to support the development of the pupil with SEND.

Early identification of developmental delay, and prompt interventions, can help to ensure that a pupil with SEND makes progress across all areas of development. Without early intervention, a SEND pupil's self-image may deteriorate, which then makes them reluctant to participate in learning and other school activities.

Further information about child development and the developmental milestones can be accessed at www.psychology.about.com and also at www.ask-nanny.com/child-development.htm.

Table 3.6

Child development developmental milestones

Age 0–3 years			
Physical development	**Cognitive development**	**Social and emotional development**	**Communication development**
By 6 months: Turn their head towards sound and movement; watch adult's face when feeding; smile at familiar faces and voices; reach up to hold feet when lying on their back; look and reach for objects; hold and shake a rattle; put everything in their mouth.	**0–3 years:** Begin to realise others are separate beings from themselves; imitate others and try out ways of behaving in play; becoming more confident but still need adult reassurance.	**0–3 months:** Respond to adults' (especially mother's) faces and voices; smile and concentrate on adult's face during feeding; very dependent on adults for reassurance and comfort; quieten when held and cuddled.	**0–3 months:** Make a variety of 'happy' sounds; respond to music and other sounds; watch the face of main carer, especially the mouth, and try to copy its movements.
6 months–1 year: Move from sitting with support to sitting alone; roll over from their stomach onto their back; begin to creep, crawl or shuffle on their bottom; pull on or push against adult hands or furniture to reach a standing position; raise arms to be lifted up; turn and look up when they hear their name; pat and poke objects when playing; pass objects from hand to hand; look for things that have been hidden or dropped; reach hand towards food sources.		**6–9 months:** Enjoy company of others and games like 'I See' and 'Peek-A-Boo'; show affection to main carer, but are shy with strangers.	**6–12 months:** Babbling sounds begin; make four or five different sounds and turn their head towards the source of sounds; show feelings by squealing with pleasure or crying; laugh and chuckle to show enjoyment.
		1–2 years: Like to please adults and to perform for an audience; may become anxious or distressed if separated from known adults; may use comfort object; mostly cooperative and can be distracted from unwanted behaviour; play alongside other children.	**1–2 years:** Move from using single words to putting them together as a simple phrase; understand key words in the sentences used; in the second year they start to understand the use of conversation and begin to copy parents/carers; children's understanding outstrips their ability to express themselves; by age 2 they may be using 30–150 words.
1–2 years: Begin to walk; sit alone indefinitely; feed themselves; push and pull toys while walking; wave goodbye; point or make noises to indicate wants; enjoy a picture book; shake head for 'No'; use thumb and first two fingers to grip; bang objects together; crawl upstairs; stoop to pick		**2–3 years:** Developing sense of own identity, wanting to do things for self; demanding of adult attention, jealous of attention given to others; reluctant to share playthings or adults' attention; act impulsively, requiring needs to be met instantly; prone to bursts of emotion and tantrums; enjoy playing with adults or older children who will	**2–3 years:** Able to put words together into a sentence; begin to ask questions (e.g. 'What?', 'Why?' etc.); can join in well-known songs or verses and put actions to words; could be using several hundred words by their third birthday; can scribble and make marks on paper with a crayon.

(continued)

Table 3.6 (continued)

Child development developmental milestones

Age 0–3 years

Physical development	Cognitive development	Social and emotional development	Communication development
things up from the floor; begin to show preference for one hand; build tower of few bricks; hold crayon in palm and make marks on paper. **2–3 years:** Kneel to play; throw; kick balls; build larger brick tower; pour liquids; use pencil to make marks and circular scribbles.		give attention; beginning to play with others of own age for short periods of time.	

Age 3–7 years

Physical development	Cognitive development	Social and emotional development	Communication development
3 years: Jump with feet together; walk on tip-toes; walk up and down stairs; catch a gently thrown ball; climb with increasing confidence; paint; thread beads on a lace; gain control over eating implements. **4 years:** Pedal; throw with aim; use scissors; hold a pencil and can draw people/ houses. **5 years:** Hop; kick with aim; catch a ball; handle a pencil with control; copy shapes and write some letters. **6–7 years:** Skip; ride bicycle; jump from height; climb confidently; write; thread a needle; can do up buttons and tie shoe laces.	**3–4 years:** Understand two or three simple things to do at once (e.g. fetch a drink, give it to a sibling and take the empty glass back to the kitchen); sort objects by size and type (e.g. by colour, by shape). **5–7 years:** Begin to understand about sameness and difference in various aspects of life; begin to understand that differences can exist side by side; begin to see different perspectives on the same subject (e.g. the same amount of water can look different in different containers).	**3–4 years:** Becoming more independent and self-motivated; feel more secure and able to cope with unfamiliar surroundings and adults for periods of time; becoming more cooperative with adults and like to help; sociable and friendly with others; play with other children and are able to share; beginning to consider the needs of others and to show concern for others. **4–7 years:** Make friends but may need help in resolving disputes and disagreements; developing an understanding of rules, but still find turn-taking difficult; enjoy helping others and taking responsibility; learn lots about the world and how it works, and about people	**3–4 years:** Start to use pitch and tone when talking; may start to use the past tense; vocabulary extends towards 1,000–1,500 words; marks made with crayons become more controlled. **4–5 years:** Grammar is becoming more accurate; questions become more complex; more able to use language to communicate their own ideas; understand that books are a source of pleasure and use pictures to help them follow the story; may begin to recognise their own name and a few frequently seen written words; can hold a pencil steadily and copy shapes and form some lettering. **5–7 years:** Fluent speakers able to make up stories;

Age 3–7 years

Physical development	Cognitive development	Social and emotional development	Communication development
		and relationships; make friends (often short-term) and play group games; need structure and a routine to feel safe; need limits to be set when behaviour is 'over the top'.	can handle books well; understand that text carries meaning; recognise an increasing number of letters linking them to sounds.

Age 7–12 years

Physical development	Cognitive development	Social and emotional development	Communication development
Run, jump, skip, hit a ball, climb and swing; enjoy playing team games by age 8; may misjudge their ability before age 9. At pre-teens: become modest about their bodies and seek privacy; may also begin to become interested in the opposite sex; compare their physical development with that of other peers around them.	Read to themselves; take a lively interest in certain subjects by age 9. As they near their teens, they are able to motivate themselves and concentrate longer, thus can work more intensely on homework. They are able to learn to plan for the completion of projects and coursework.	Becoming less dependent on close adults for support (able to cope with wider environment); enjoy being in groups of other children of similar age and are strongly influenced by their peer group; becoming more aware of their own gender; developing understanding that certain kinds of behaviour are not acceptable and why; developing a strong sense of fairness and justice (understand right from wrong); want to fit in with peer group rules; at age 12 some encounter peer group pressure and find it hard to resist trying out smoking and/or drinking alcohol; sensitive to others' opinions about them; start to form closer friendships at about age 8; like to play with same-sex friends; need adult help to sort out arguments and disagreements in play with peers; can be arrogant and bossy or shy and uncertain.	Need help in tackling the complexities of spelling; vocabulary will grow if adults introduce new words and new ways of using language; speak fluently and describe complicated happenings; read out loud; know the different tenses and grammar.

(continued)

Table 3.6 (continued)

Child development developmental milestones

Adolescence (age 12–19 years)

Physical development	Cognitive development	Social and emotional development	Communication development
Overall, during adolescence, coordination and strength increase greatly; by the age of 19 or 20, the adolescent has full adult motor capacities.	Cognitive development is uneven and affected by emotions.	**Social development 12–14 years:** Psychologically distance themselves from parents; identify with peer group; social status is largely related to group membership; social acceptance depends on conformity to observable traits or roles; need to be independent from all adults; ambivalent about sexual relationships, and sexual behaviour is exploratory.	Use sarcasm and wit often, as they test out their new sophisticated language skills; develop an interest in satire and other slightly off-beat forms of humour; their logical thinking ability is also maturing and they may enjoy practising their new intellectual and verbal skills through informal discussion and formal debating; voice their opinions on current events, and on popular or controversial topics.
Boys Adolescence in boys begins later than in girls (around 14 years). Boys begin to develop deeper voices, body hair and muscle growth, as well as testicle and scrotum growth in mid-puberty. Boys go through puberty between the ages of 12 and 15. Boys have the greatest growth spurt between the ages of 13 and 17.	They can calculate consequences of thoughts and actions without experiencing them; can make connections between knowledge and practical application in daily life; are able to think logically (can identify and reject hypotheses or possible outcomes based on logic); are able to think about thought (which leads to introspection and self-analysis); understand and consider others' perspectives and perspectives of the social system; can tackle a problem, consider multiple solutions and plan a course of action.	**Social development 15–19 years:** Friendships are based on loyalty, understanding and trust; conscious choices are made about which adults to trust; some may become sexually active.	
Girls Girls go through puberty between the ages of 11 and 14. Girls' breasts begin to swell; pubic hair grows darker and curlier. By 13, some girls are almost physically mature, with the onset of menstruation occurring at 13. Some girls have reached full physical maturity by the age of 14 or 15. Girls have the greatest growth spurt between the ages of 11 and 14.		**Emotional development 12–14 years:** Self-conscious about changes in their physical appearance; may over-react to parental questions or criticisms; enjoy engaging in activities for intense emotional experience; some may engage in risky behaviour; reliance on peer group for support. **Emotional development 14–19 years:** Emotional maturity shifts between childish needs and adult desires; positive self-image; examine beliefs and values of others.	

Questions for reflection

1 A pupil with Down's Syndrome (SLD) has recently joined your class. Developmentally, they are operating at a level three years below their peers. Describe the approaches you will use to differentiate the curriculum, in order to make it accessible for the pupil concerned.

2 Which aspect of high-quality teaching poses the greatest challenge to you, in relation to meeting the needs of a diversity of pupils with SEND in your class? Describe how you will develop this aspect of your teaching further.

3 You notice that a pupil with speech, language and communication needs does not appear to be accessing the curriculum sufficiently in your lesson. Identify the possible barriers to learning that they may be experiencing, and describe the approaches you will use to minimise and remove them.

4 Which aspect of high-incidence SEND presents a challenge for you, and how will you go about addressing the issue?

5 The government considers that the needs of the majority of pupils with high-incidence SEND can be met through high-quality teaching, which is differentiated and personalised. How far do you agree or disagree with this view?

CHAPTER 4

Making accurate and productive use of assessment

This chapter covers:

- The underpinning principles of assessment

- The purpose of assessment

- Assessment terminology

- The government's latest assessment expectations and reforms

- The draft 2014 *SEND Code of Practice* and assessment

- The principles and practice of effective AfL and pupils with SEND

- How best to give pupils with SEND assessment feedback

- Using and analysing SEND pupil-level attainment data

- How to engage pupils with SEND in assessing and reviewing their own learning

The underpinning principles of assessment

On 13 February 2014, the National Association of Head Teachers (NAHT) published the findings of its Commission into Assessment without Levels. In their report, they made several recommendations for supporting schools in determining new assessment arrangements in relation to the revised national curriculum and pupils' learning. The NAHT Commission also identified a set of key national principles for good assessment that would help the adoption of a more consistent approach to assessment in schools across the country. These underpinning principles can be found on p. 8 of the NAHT report, and Table 4.1 in this chapter provides a useful overview of what each principle entails.

The DfE identifies the following principles upon which their assessment reforms are based:

- Ongoing, teacher-led assessment is a crucial part of effective teaching.

- Schools should have the freedom to decide how to teach their curriculum and how to track the progress that pupils make.

- Both summative teacher assessment and external testing are important.

- Accountability is key to a successful school system, and therefore must be fair and transparent.

Table 4.1

NAHT underpinning principles for assessment in schools

1. Assessment is at the heart of teaching and learning because it:	a. provides evidence to guide teaching and learning; b. provides the opportunity for pupils to demonstrate and review their progress.
2. Assessment is fair because it:	a. is inclusive of all abilities; b. is free from bias towards factors that are not relevant to what the assessment intends to address.
3. Assessment is honest because assessment:	a. outcomes are used in ways that minimise undesirable effects; b. outcomes are conveyed in an open, honest and transparent way to assist pupils with their learning; c. judgements are moderated by experienced professionals to ensure their accuracy.
4. Assessment is ambitious because:	a. it places achievement in context against nationally standardised criteria and expected standards; b. it embodies, through objective criteria, a pathway of progress and development for every pupil; c. its objectives set high expectations for pupils as learners.
5. Assessment is appropriate because:	a. the purpose of any assessment process is clearly stated; b. conclusions regarding pupil achievement are valid when the assessment method is appropriate to the age of the pupil, to the task and to the desired feedback information; c. it draws on a wide range of evidence to provide a complete picture of pupil achievement; d. achievement demands no more procedures or records than are practically required to allow pupils, their parents and teachers to plan future learning.
6. Assessment is consistent because:	a. judgements are formed according to common principles; b. the results are readily understandable by third parties; c. the school's results are capable of comparison with other schools, both locally and nationally.
7. Assessment outcomes provide meaningful and understandable information for:	a. pupils, in developing their learning; b. parents, in supporting their child with their learning; c. teachers, in planning teaching and learning – assessment provides information that justifies the time spent; d. school leaders and governors, in planning and allocating resources; e. government, and agents of the government.
8. Assessment feedback should inspire greater effort and a belief that:	a. through hard work and practice, more can be achieved.

(Source: NAHT 2014: 8)

- Measures of both progress and attainment are important for understanding school performance.
- A broad range of information should be published to help parents, carers and the wider public to know how well schools are performing (DfE 2014c: 4).

The purpose of assessment

The purpose of assessment is to:

- inform pupils, parents and carers, governors and teachers about pupil performance, with a view to improving teaching and learning;

- hold schools to account for the attainment and progress of all pupils;

- enable benchmarking between schools, academy chains and federations, in addition to monitoring performance both locally and nationally;

- award external qualifications such as GCSE, EBacc, A Levels and vocational qualifications.

The links between curriculum, assessment and pedagogy are important and an effective assessment system, built around a revised curriculum, helps to inform classroom practice and improve teaching and learning.

The NAHT identified that further work needed to be undertaken to improve the training for assessment within ITT, the NQT induction year and ongoing professional development, in order to build assessment capacity and strengthen practice within the school system. The NAHT Commission's report on assessment stated:

> All those responsible for children's learning should undertake rigorous training in formative, diagnostic and summative assessment, which covers how assessment can be used to support teaching and learning for all pupils, including those with special educational needs.
>
> (NAHT 2014: 7.16)

The DfE has provided additional funding to teaching schools to enable them to help and support schools in their alliances, to prepare for the new assessment arrangements, which can include offering CPD in assessment for qualified, newly qualified and trainee teachers.

The DfE has set up a small innovation fund to enable schools to share new assessment systems and assessment processes on a much wider basis. Schools that have good and outstanding practice in the area of assessment (e.g. effective model assessment systems, assessment case studies, examples of what good assessment looks like) can apply for the assessment innovation award. The DfE will make this best practice in assessment available online throughout 2014 and 2015 for other schools to access and use.

Assessment terminology

- **Assessment**, as part of everyday teaching, is used to denote a range of measurement functions for formative, diagnostic and summative uses. Assessment is not an exact science. Teachers assess pupils' progress on an ongoing basis in the classroom, determining what is being learned, what pupils know, understand and can do, and what they need to do next in order to make progress, as part of formative and/or diagnostic assessment.

- **Diagnostic assessment** looks backwards, as it assesses what the pupil already knows and/or identifies the nature of learning difficulties and barriers to learning. It can also be referred to as 'pre-assessment', as it also helps to identify any gaps or misconceptions existing in a pupil's learning.

- **Formative assessment** refers to the ongoing assessment of a pupil's progress that takes place at regular intervals, with accompanying feedback, to help them to improve upon their current performance.

- **Summative assessment** refers to the summary of a pupil's overall learning or final achievement and level of understanding at the end of an academic year, Key Stage or course of study, which usually involves the pupil taking a standardised test or an external examination.

- **P levels** are differentiated performance criteria used for assessing the attainment of pupils with SEND aged five to sixteen, who are working below national curriculum Level 1 and who have more complex and severe special educational needs (e.g. PMLD, SLD and MLD). As part of moderated summative teacher assessment, the P levels provide a 'best-fit' judgement, aligned to the updated and revised P level 2014 national curriculum subject descriptors. The P levels are comprised of eight graduated smaller-stepped performance levels, P1 to P8. Levels P1 to P3 relate to early levels of general attainment, and Levels P4 to P8 relate to subject-specific performance. P levels help to track linear and lateral progress, as well as informing target setting for pupils with the most complex and severe SEND.

The government's latest assessment expectations and reforms

Whether you are an experienced qualified teacher, an NQT or a trainee teacher, it is helpful to have an overview of the government's latest reforms on assessment and accountability, in light of the new national curriculum.

The DfE is removing the reliance on national curriculum levels to judge pupils' progress at the end of Key Stages 1 and 2, and is introducing more challenging tests that will report a precise scaled score, rather than a level. A scaled score is a score where 100 will represent the new expected standard for that stage.

The government considers that national curriculum attainment levels have become too abstract and ambiguous over the past few years, in not giving parents and carers meaningful information as to how their child is performing and not informing pupils about how to improve. In their place will be more detailed performance descriptors that directly link to the content of the new national curriculum. These will help to inform teacher assessment at the end of Key Stages 1, 2 and 3 by enabling teachers to record a pupil's attainment against each applicable assessment criterion. The criteria provide a qualitative statement of achievement and each pupil will be assessed as either 'developing', 'meeting' or 'exceeding' each relevant criterion.

At the end of Key Stage 4, the new grading system for GCSEs will see an extra grade being introduced by 2017. An overview of the new GCSE grading system is illustrated in Figure 4.1.

Table 4.2 provides a summary of the government's overall new assessment and accountability reforms in the primary and secondary phases of education, which will become effective from 2016.

Table 4.2

Government assessment and accountability reforms effective from 2016

Early Years Foundation Stage (EYFS) & Primary phase	Secondary phase & 16–19

EYFS

Early Years Foundation Stage Profile no longer compulsory from September 2016.

Statutory Progress Check for those aged between 2 to 3, focusing on communication and language, physical development, and personal, social and emotional development.

From September 2015 the Healthy Child Programme review at age 2 to check the physical development milestones will be combined with the Statutory Progress Check to form one integrated review at age 2–3.

Floor Standard – end of Key Stage 2

DfE minimum requirement that 85 per cent of children will make sufficient progress from their starting point in Reception baseline to the end of Key Stage 2 (e.g. equivalent to at least national curriculum level 4b in all reading, writing and maths) to meet the new expected standard.

RECEPTION

New age-appropriate **Reception Baseline** fully implemented in September 2016 to be taken by children within the first few weeks at school, which is supplemented by teachers' broader formative assessments and observations.

KEY STAGE 3

DfE no longer collect Key Stage 3 teacher assessment results, and DfE will not prescribe a national system for schools' ongoing assessment at Key Stage 3. It is up to schools to decide how they assess each national curriculum subject at Key Stage 3. Schools will be expected to track pupil progress, make accurate assessments to support learning and report to parents/carers at Key Stage 3 on pupil progress (i.e. whether their child is working towards, meets or exceeds the new national curriculum performance descriptors for each subject).

Floor Standard – end of Key Stage 4

DfE set floor standard as being the progress made by pupils from the end of Key Stage 2 to their score across a suite of eight subjects at the end of Key Stage 4, known as the Progress 8 measure. A school will be below the floor standard if progress is 0.5 grades less than expected across eight subjects. Where this is the case, an Ofsted inspection will be triggered.

KEY STAGE 4

KS4 Progress 8 measure 2016:

Schools will be held accountable for pupils' progress in a suite of eight qualifications: English, Maths, three EBacc subjects, then an 'open' group of subjects which includes EBacc subjects not already counted in the specific EBacc slot, and other high-value academic, arts and vocational qualifications.

Where a pupil has not taken the maximum number of qualifications that count in each group, they will receive a zero point score for that empty slot.

2016 point scores

The Progress 8 point score scale will change from 16–58 to become a 1–8 point scale where each GCSE grade represents one point. Thus Grade G = 1 point, and Grade A* = 8 points.

2017 point scores

A new 1–9 point score scale for GCSEs will be introduced in 2017, which will take account of the new GCSEs. Grades GCSE F/G = 1 point, up to Grade A* = 9 points.

(Figure 4.1 illustrates the full 2017 point scale).

KEY STAGE 1

Phonics check at the end of Year 1.

End of Key Stage 1: Teacher assessment in maths and reading informed by externally set, internally marked tests.

In addition, there will be an externally set test in grammar, punctuation and spelling, which will help to inform teacher assessment of writing.

The Key Stage 1 updated and more challenging tests reflect the new national curriculum, and results are expressed as a scaled score rather than as a level. These new assessments will first take place in summer 2016.

Teacher assessment of speaking and listening and science will continue.

From autumn 2014, new performance descriptors are introduced to inform statutory teacher assessments at the end of Key Stage 1. For maths, reading, writing and speaking and listening, teachers assess pupils as meeting one of several performance descriptors. For science, there is only a single performance descriptor of the new expected standard. These are linked to the content of the new curriculum.

Teacher assessment will be moderated to ensure validity and reliability.

KEY STAGE 2

End of Key Stage 2: Pupils continue to sit more challenging externally set and marked tests in maths, reading and grammar, punctuation and spelling. These will be used for school performance measures from 2016 onwards.

Teacher assessment in maths, reading, writing and science will continue to give a broader picture of a child's attainment. The tests and assessments will reflect the content of the new curriculum.

New performance descriptors introduced to inform statutory teacher assessments at the end of Key Stage 2. For writing, teachers assess pupils as meeting one of several performance descriptors. For science, reading and maths there is a single performance descriptor of the new expected standard. A sample of pupils will continue to sit tests in science to give a picture of national performance.

Teacher assessment will be moderated to ensure validity and reliability.

The results of the tests in reading, maths, and grammar, punctuation and spelling are reported to pupils and parents/carers as scaled scores. Parents/carers will be provided with their child's score alongside the average for their school, the local area and nationally.

16–19

DfE introduced headline measures of performance for all 16–19 providers, which include:

– progress measures;
– attainment measures;
– retention measures;
– English and Maths progress measures for those who did not achieve good grades at age 16;
– destination measures.

(Source: Adapted from DfE 2014c and DfE 2013c)

Grade 9: Top A* performers

Grade 8: Those who obtained an A* at the lower end, but did not qualify for a 9

Grade 7: The equivalent of a grade A

Grade 6: This will cover those from two-thirds above current C grade to top of existing B grade

Grade 5: International benchmark – showing performance equals that of those getting top grade passes in international league tables (half or two-thirds of a grade above current C pass)

Grade 4: Equivalent to a C grade

Grade 3: C/D borderline

Grade 2: Equivalent to D and E grades

Grade 1: Equivalent to F and G grades

Figure 4.1 New GCSE grading system effective from 2017

Government guidance relating to assessment and pupils with SEND

The primary and secondary phase government guidance in relation to the revised assessment reforms and lower-attaining pupils with more complex and severe SEND, who are unable to access the relevant end-of-Key-Stage test or enter any GCSEs or high-value vocational qualifications in order to meet the Progress 8 measure at the end of Key Stage 4, recommends that these pupils should continue to have their attainment assessed by teachers. This is why the P levels are being retained – to enable teachers to report their judgements relating to the performance of SEND pupils with PMLD, SLD and MLD.

Given the diverse nature of pupils with SEND, pupil-level attainment data for these children needs to be viewed and analysed in context to give a clear picture of their performance and progress. For example, class and subject teachers, when analysing the attainment data for these pupils, will need to take into account the following contextual factors:

- the nature and complexity of the pupil's SEND;
- the nature and number of additional interventions they access;
- whether they are a summer birth;
- their gender;
- their school attendance record (e.g. if this has been affected by medical issues or because they have been a victim of bullying);
- the number and nature of any school exclusions;
- their ethnicity;
- whether they also have EAL;
- whether they are an LAC;
- whether they are on FSM;
- whether they are a pupil premium child;
- socio-economic background (e.g. level of deprivation, from a one-parent family, or living within a vulnerable family in crisis or workless).

Trainee and qualified teachers may find it useful to refer to the following DfE documents relating to the new assessment and accountability reforms:

- *Reforming the Accountability System for Secondary Schools: Government Response to the February to May 2013 Consultation on Secondary School Accountability. October 2013* (DfE 2013c);

- *Reforming Assessment and Accountability for Primary Schools: Government Response to Consultation on Primary School Assessment and Accountability. March 2014* (DfE 2014c);

- *National Curriculum and Assessment from September 2014: Information for Schools* (DfE 2014j);

- *Update on Progress 8 Measure and Reforms to Secondary School Accountability Framework. January 2014* (DfE 2014m);

- *Progress 8 Measure in 2016: Technical Guide for Maintained Secondary Schools, Academies and Free Schools. March 2014* (DfE 2014n).

All of the above DfE publications are available to download from www.gov.uk/government/uploads.

In April 2014, the Office for Qualifications and Examinations Regulation (Ofqual) published a useful document relating to the assessment at the end of Key Stage 4 entitled *Consultation on Setting the Grade Standards of New GCSEs in England*, which can be downloaded from www.ofqual.gov.uk.

The draft 2014 *SEND Code of Practice* and assessment

The draft 2014 *SEND Code of Practice* expects that:

> Class and subject teachers, supported by the senior leadership team, should make regular assessments of progress for all pupils. These should seek to identify pupils making less than expected progress given their age and individual circumstances. This can be characterised by progress that:
>
> - is significantly slower than that of their peers starting from the same baseline;
> - fails to match or better the child's previous rate of progress;
> - fails to close the attainment gap between the child and their peers;
> - widens the attainment gap.
>
> (DfE 2014g: 6.14)

Later, the draft 2014 *SEND Code of Practice* further advises: 'Where progress continues to be less than expected the class or subject teacher, working with the SENCO, should assess whether the child has SEN' (DfE 2014g: 6.16). This further assessment is the first step in the four-part cycle of the graduated approach for delivering SEN Support to those pupils who do not have an EHC plan (see Chapter 2).

The principles and practice of effective AfL and pupils with SEND

AfL, as part of high-quality teaching, is comprised of two main phases:

1 initial or diagnostic assessment; and

2 formative assessment.

AfL is the process of seeking and interpreting evidence for use by pupils and their teachers to decide where the pupil is in their learning, what strengths the pupil has in a topic or subject, the areas where further improvement is required, where to go next in learning and how best to get there. AfL enables teachers to adjust their teaching to keep pupils with SEND on track.

AfL occurs throughout the learning process from the start of a unit of work or course of study to the end stage of summative assessment. It aims to encourage pupils with SEND to be more active in their learning and associated assessment. Teachers need to know at the outset of a unit of work or course of study where the pupil with SEND is in terms of their prior and current learning in a subject. AfL not only enables teachers to continually check on how pupils with SEND are progressing in their learning, but also strengthens the feedback they get from those pupils in relation to what they know, understand and can do in a subject area.

AfL uses a range of information sources, such as teacher observation, discussion about learning with pupils and with other colleagues, the marking of written work and portfolios of work.

Using AfL helps to guide classroom practice for all pupils, including those with SEND, because it:

- informs planning for teaching and learning and enables teaching and learning support to be tailored and adjusted, by taking account of assessment results;
- focuses on knowing how pupils learn;
- actively involves pupils in their own learning;
- builds pupils' self-esteem and enhances their motivation to learn;
- supports pupils' self-assessment and peer assessment, helping them to know how to improve;
- provides a vehicle for giving pupils feedback on their learning and work;
- enables pupils to take greater responsibility and ownership for their own progress.

Effective daily assessment for learning strategies to use with pupils with SEND can include:

- using prompting and probing questions to assess pupils' understanding by giving pupils with SEND extra thinking time to respond to questions;
- making planned observations of pupils with SEND during teaching and learning so as to help to identify any barriers to learning and participation;
- holding focused discussions with pupils with SEND about their work and learning, to enable them to reflect upon their progress and articulate successes against targets set;
- analysing SEND pupils' work and giving them constructive feedback to guide further improvement;
- engaging pupils with SEND in the AfL process through the use of paired peer assessment, to promote discussion and reflection on the learning strategies used.

How best to give pupils with SEND assessment feedback

When giving pupils with SEND constructive oral feedback on their work, it is important to use positive language when they find a task difficult. For example, 'It's making you think because you are learning something new.'

AfL enables trainee and qualified teachers to identify:

- what helps or hinders SEND pupils' access to the curriculum and learning;
- the impact of their teaching on the learning of pupils with SEND;
- the strengths and talents that pupils with SEND have;
- the gaps, misconceptions and misunderstandings that pupils with SEND may have in their learning;
- appropriate and relevant learning targets;
- the pupils' views of their own learning strengths and weaknesses.

Table 4.3 offers useful strategies to support AfL with SEND pupils.

Using and analysing SEND pupil-level attainment data

The effective use and analysis of SEND pupil-level attainment data helps to inform improvement in the quality and effectiveness of teaching and learning for this group of pupils. Assessing and analysing the achievements of pupils with SEND over time are essential elements in developing a more 'forensic' approach to removing barriers to learning, raising expectations and supporting the setting of realistic and stretching targets for pupils with SEND.

The analysis of SEND pupil-level attainment data can provide a deeper understanding of the performance of individuals and groups of pupils with SEND over time. It helps to inform which additional and different interventions and teaching approaches are the most effective in ensuring that pupils with SEND make the expected progress. SEND pupil-level attainment data analysis also offers teachers a better understanding of the impact that high-quality differentiated and personalised teaching and additional interventions have on SEND pupils' learning outcomes. Effective interpretation of moderated teacher assessment and test outcomes helps to further tailor teaching and learning for pupils with SEND at the classroom level.

Class and subject teachers will find it helpful to reflect on the following aspects, in relation to using and analysing SEND pupil-level attainment data:

- the criteria being used to determine whether pupils with SEND are underachieving;
- the strategies and approaches being used to address any SEND pupil underachievement and to narrow the attainment gap;
- the key national indicators and national data sets being used, which aid comparative analysis of SEND pupil progress (e.g. the revised DfE Progression data sets, RAISEonline and Fischer Family Trust (FFT) analysis reports, all aligned to the changes in the new national curriculum assessment reforms);
- the in-house systems and approaches being used across the school to assess, target set and evaluate the rates of progress that pupils with SEND make;

Table 4.3

Useful strategies for supporting AfL with pupils with SEND

Key characteristics of AfL	Strategies to use with pupils with SEND
Sharing the learning objectives with the pupils	– Share learning objectives at the beginning of lessons and at various points throughout, in language that the pupils with SEND will understand. – Use the objectives as the basis for targeted questioning during the lesson and in plenaries. – Relate the learning to the 'big picture' of the topic.
Helping pupils to know and recognise the standards for which they are aiming	– Show pupils work that has met assessment criteria and explain why. – Model what the work should look and sound like. – Explain what you are looking for, using clear success criteria, and relate this to the learning objectives. – Ensure that there are clear expectations about the pupils' presentation of work. – Provide displays that show 'work in progress' as well as finished pieces. – Have prompts for success criteria on posters or in the backs of books.
Involving pupils in peer and self-assessment	– Give pupils opportunities to talk about what they have learned and what they have found difficult with reference to the learning objectives. – Encourage pupils to discuss their work together, focusing on how to improve. – Ask pupils to explain their thinking and reasoning. – Give time for pupils to reflect on their learning together.
Providing feedback that leads pupils to recognise their next steps and how to take them	– Give value via positive and specific oral feedback. – In marking, relate to the assessment success criteria: identify what the pupil has done.
Promoting confidence that every pupil can improve	– To boost confidence, identify the small steps so that pupils can see their progress for themselves. – Develop an ethos of support and encouragement among the class.
Involving both the teacher and pupil in reviewing and reflecting on assessment information	– Reflect with pupils on their work and the learning processes involved. – Reward efforts to contribute and think about what learning has been gained in the lesson.

(Source: DfES 2005: 15)

- what constitutes good and outstanding progress for pupils with SEND within the school, which takes account of linear and lateral progress;
- the effectiveness of moderated teacher assessment within and beyond the school, across the curriculum, in order to ensure that valid judgements are made about the attainment and progress of pupils with SEND, thereby helping to identify strengths and gaps in subject coverage, or aspects of subject teaching that require further development and improvement.

Trainee teachers and NQTs unsure about the government's new assessment procedures and reforms would be well advised to book some quality time with the assessment coordinator in the school, in order to be guided through how to interpret and inter-rogate SEND pupil-level attainment data in the school's specific RAISEonline and FFT reports, in addition to the national DfE Progression data sets and the school's own internal pupil-level attainment data, in order to:

- contribute evidence to the whole-school self-evaluation process, in judging how well pupils with SEND are progressing across the curriculum;
- evaluate the progress towards meeting the targets set for pupils with SEND;
- make informed decisions about the most effective deployment of TAs to enhance and extend the learning of pupils with SEND;
- evaluate the impact of additional and different provision for pupils with SEND;
- identify trends over three years in the attainment of pupils with SEND;
- compare the school's SEND pupils' performance in national curriculum subjects with that of similar schools locally and nationally;
- identify any gaps existing in SEND pupils' learning in an aspect of a subject;
- identify any cohorts or groups of pupils with SEND who may be underachieving.

Trainee, class and subject teachers may also find it helpful to book a session with the school's SENCO to guide them through the use of the DfE revised Progression data sets.

What SEND data should teachers be using and analysing?

Class and subject teachers need to gather qualitative as well as quantitative evidence, in order to gain a secure view about the progress of pupils with SEND. The following questions provide some useful prompts for teachers:

- What does my SEND pupil data tracking tell me about the progress and achieve-ments of these pupils in my subject area? Is it good enough?
- What are the SEND pupils' views about their progress?
- What are the views of the SENCO, the TA and any other external profession-als working with the SEND pupils on the progress of these pupils in my subject area/class?
- What do my and others' observations of my lessons indicate about SEND pupils' progress in their learning in my subject area?
- What does my scrutiny of SEND pupils' work tell me about their learning and progress, and about the effectiveness of my teaching?

Teachers will find the following types of data useful in analysing the outcomes of SEND pupils as learners:

- value-added data that compares the difference between pupils' actual results and their expected results at the end of a Key Stage;

- attendance data, particularly as poor attendance impacts on pupils' learning outcomes;

- exclusions data (fixed-term and permanent exclusions), as again exclusions can impact negatively on SEND pupils' learning;

- rewards and sanctions data including behaviour data, which influences the self-esteem, attitudes and motivation of SEND pupils as learners;

- well-being data (e.g. Health Related Behaviour Questionnaire (HRBQ), Pupil Attitude to Self and School (PASS)), as poor well-being impacts negatively on SEND pupils' ability to learn effectively.

Analysis of all the above pupil-level data helps class and subject teachers to gain a more holistic picture and a greater insight into why some pupils with SEND may be underachieving and not making the expected rate of progress.

Understanding RAISEonline and FFT data

RAISEonline and FFT are two data packages used by schools, LAs and Ofsted inspectors. Both resources use data gathered from the School Census to compare attainment and progress linked to levels of interventions for pupils on SEN Support and with EHC plans.

Class and subject teachers are expected to be able to use and analyse pupil-level data in both packages, as well as interpret and compare their school-level SEND pupil outcomes in a curriculum area with other local and national data sets for pupils with SEND.

Further resources on assessment

The RAISEonline document library (www.raiseonline.org/documentlibrary/) is worth browsing, to keep up to date with any changes to the Transition Matrices, and to the Summary Reports.

The DfE publication entitled *Progression 2010–11*, with accompanying data sets, can be downloaded from www.gov.uk/government/uploads.

The National Governors' Association website (www.nga.org.uk) offers downloadable resources that may also be of interest to those teachers who value a more user-friendly guide to understanding and interpreting data:

- *Knowing Your School: RAISEonline for Governors of Primary Schools*, second edition, January 2014 (NGA 2014a);

- *Knowing Your School: RAISEonline for Governors of Secondary Schools*, second edition, January 2014 (NGA 2014b);

- *Knowing Your School: The FFT Governor Dashboard for Primary School Governors*, May 2013 (NGA 2013a);

- *Knowing Your School: The FFT Governor Dashboard for Secondary School Governors*, May 2013 (NGA 2013b).

Online guidance on how to navigate and interpret FFT data can be accessed at www.fischertrust.org.

However, teachers need to take into account that the NGA publications listed above and the RAISEonline and FFT data were based on data from the previous national curriculum, implemented from September 2014. They will therefore need to look out for information regarding future changes in light of the new national curriculum revised assessment system.

How to engage pupils with SEND in assessing and reviewing their own learning

The following assessment approaches can help pupils with SEND, who find oral communication difficult, to assess their own work and that of another peer:

- Use of traffic light colours to highlight their work: red means pupils have not achieved the task and feel confused; amber means they feel they have made some progress, but are uncertain about certain things/aspects; green means they have achieved the task and feel confident.

- Use of thumbs as a sign of achievement and understanding: thumbs down means they are struggling with the work, are unclear about what to do and would welcome help; thumbs sideways means they think they are OK but are not sure and their work might need checking; and thumbs up means they understand the work and feel they are doing well.

- The teacher's use of prompt questions and statements that are displayed on the classroom wall or are on individual cards: 'What areas of your work do you think could be improved and how/why?', 'What did you find the hardest to do and where can you get further help?', 'What are we learning to (WALT) . . .?', 'What I'm looking for (WILF) in the work/lesson is . . .', 'This is because (TIB) . . .'. 'The three things I have learnt in today's lesson are . . .'.

- Examples of what a particular national curriculum or P level subject descriptor looks like in anonymous pieces of work.

Questions for reflection

1 In view of the government's assessment and accountability reforms, what will be your first priority in relation to assessing the achievements of pupils with SEND robustly?

2 Describe the practical steps you could take in supporting a pupil with communication and interaction difficulties to assess their own work.

3 In what ways could you further improve your current system for tracking and analysing the attainment of pupils with SEND in your class or subject area, in order to make it more pupil- and parent-/carer-friendly?

4 How would you tailor your current assessment system to make the comparison of outcomes for those pupils on SEN Support and those with an EHC plan easier to interpret and analyse?

continued

5 You have been allocated a session with the school's SENCO to discuss how best to moderate your teacher assessment on the achievements of pupils with SEND. What three questions would you wish to explore further with the SENCO that would help you to improve this aspect of your assessment practice?

CHAPTER 5

Effective behaviour management to ensure a good and safe learning environment

This chapter covers:

- Identification of pupils with social, emotional and mental health difficulties
- The government's expectations regarding pupil behaviour
- Different levels of classroom behaviour
- Recording, analysing and tracking pupil behaviour
- The four Rs framework for effective behaviour management
- Twenty top tips for managing pupil behaviour
- Meeting Ofsted's expectations for pupil behaviour
- Identifying and tackling bullying, including cyber-bullying
- Identifying and tackling low self-esteem
- Developing a safe and emotionally intelligent learning environment
- Further useful resources

Identification of pupils with social, emotional and mental health difficulties

The draft 2014 *SEND Code of Practice* has replaced the term 'behavioural, emotional and social difficulties' (BESD) with 'social, emotional and mental health difficulties'. These pupils will have a continuum of persistent needs, irrespective of ability. Pupils who have difficulties with their emotional and social development tend to have immature social skills, and they find it difficult to make and sustain positive relationships and lasting friendships with their peers. As a result, some pupils may become withdrawn or iso-lated from their peers, while others may manifest challenging, disruptive or disturbing behaviour in the classroom. The teacher needs to be aware that some of these pupils may experience mood swings, anxiety, depression, conduct problems and aggression. For some pupils, the nature of their SEND (e.g. those with autistic spectrum disorder

(ASD), or those with attention deficit hyperactive disorder (ADHD) or attention deficit disorder (ADD)) means they genuinely find it difficult to manage their own behaviour without additional support. Similarly, the side effects of their medication can result in behaviour problems (e.g. feeling tired and not wishing to work, having difficulty concentrating and becoming frustrated in their learning). All of these pupils require class and subject teachers to have clear expectations for pupil behaviour, and consistent behaviour management structures and systems in place, to enable pupils to develop self-help strategies for managing their own behaviour and emotions.

In addition, teachers are expected to make 'reasonable adjustments', under the Equality Act 2010, to ensure that these pupils can access the curriculum and participate fully in learning, while also ensuring that any resulting disruptive behaviour does not have an adverse effect on other pupils in the classroom.

Why may pupils have social, emotional and mental health difficulties?

Pupils may have social, mental and emotional health difficulties for any, or all, of the following reasons:

- **family circumstances:** due to child abuse, neglect or deprivation; family break-up, such as parents divorcing or separating; family illness or bereavement;

- **within-child factors:** due to a lack of self-confidence or low self-esteem; poor social skills; sensory/physical impairment; SpLD; tiredness;

- **school factors:** due to an inappropriate curriculum offer; ineffective rewards system, inflexible timetabling; ineffective whole-school behaviour policy that is not implemented consistently;

- **classroom factors:** due to a mismatch between curriculum delivery and pupils' learning styles; lessons being too long; insufficient curriculum differentiation; insufficient challenge in learning activities; unclear teacher instructions or explanations; poorly planned lessons; too much didactic teaching; little pupil participation in learning; inappropriate pupil groupings or seating arrangements in the classroom.

The government's expectations regarding pupil behaviour

The government's top priority is to ensure 'good behaviour' in schools, because it is seen as being central to closing the attainment gap between disadvantaged pupils and their peers. In order to support their priority, the government has:

- strengthened teachers' powers to discipline pupils;

- simplified the DfE's advice to schools on disciplining pupils, to make it clearer to teachers what they can do;

- made schools more accountable for their effectiveness in managing behaviour and tackling bullying, through the Ofsted inspection process.

Annually, the National Foundation for Educational Research (NFER) undertake a teacher survey on pupil behaviour on behalf of the DfE. The *NFER Teacher Voice Omnibus February 2012 Survey: Pupil Behaviour* (DfE 2012a), which surveyed 1,600 teachers from a range of schools across the country, found that the most frequently used behaviour management strategies used by teachers included:

- praising the behaviour teachers want to see more of among pupils;
- having a system in place to follow through with all behaviour sanctions;
- using a positive rewards system;
- displaying the classroom rules (used largely in primary schools);
- giving detention after school (used largely in secondary schools);
- giving feedback to parents and carers (positive and negative) about their child's behaviour (used more in primary schools);
- using a classroom seating plan;
- having a plan in place for pupils who are likely to misbehave.

The *NFER Teacher Voice Omnibus May 2013 Survey: Pupil Behaviour* (DfE 2013g), which sampled 1,700 teachers from a range of schools across the country, found that:

- Teachers needed to be made more aware of the DfE's updated advice relating to their powers to discipline pupils.
- Same-day detentions are being used, largely by secondary schools.
- Schools have some level of ban or limitation on pupils' use of mobile phones on school premises.
- Teachers would use physical means to break up a fight between pupils; however, only a third of teachers surveyed would use physical means to remove a disruptive pupil from the classroom.
- Just over half of the teachers surveyed felt that parents and carers generally respect a teacher's authority to discipline pupils.
- Teachers considered that the most common factors causing poor pupil behaviour in schools (excluding SEND and medical factors) were:
  - a lack of support from parents and carers;
  - poor parenting skills;
  - pupils and families with low aspirations;
  - negative cultural and media influences on children;
  - socio-economic factors;
  - pupils coming to school not ready to learn in the mornings;
  - failure to intervene early, if there is an issue regarding pupil behaviour.

The DfE's revised guidance on behaviour and discipline in schools, published in February 2014 and entitled *Behaviour and Discipline in Schools: Advice for Headteachers and School Staff*, confirmed teachers' statutory authority to discipline pupils:

- Teachers have statutory authority to discipline pupils whose behaviour is unacceptable, who break the school rules or who fail to follow a reasonable instruction (Section 90 and 91 of the Education and Inspections Act 2006).
- Teachers can discipline pupils at any time they are in school or elsewhere under the charge of a teacher, including on a school visit.
- Teachers can also discipline pupils in certain circumstances when their misbehaviour occurs outside of school (e.g. on the school bus or outside the school gates).

- Teachers have the power to impose detention outside school hours.
- Teachers can confiscate pupils' property (DfE 2014b: 6).

Teachers and trainee teachers may also value knowing what the latest DfE information states about the range of disciplinary measures a teacher can use. These include some that are already reflected in the NFER's survey findings:

- a verbal reprimand;
- extra work or repeating unsatisfactory work;
- the setting of written tasks as punishments (e.g. writing lines or an essay);
- the loss of privileges (e.g. not being able to participate in a school event, or the loss of a prized responsibility);
- missing break time with friends;
- detention at lunchtime, after school or at weekends;
- school-based community service or the imposition of a task (e.g. litter picking, weeding the school grounds, tidying a classroom, helping to clear up the dining hall after meal times, removing graffiti);
- regular reporting including morning reporting, scheduled uniform and behaviour checks, or being placed 'on report' for behaviour monitoring;
- extra physical activity (e.g. running around the school playing field or grounds); and
- in more extreme cases, temporary or permanent exclusion. (DfE 2014b: 8)

For those wishing to view the full DfE document, it can be downloaded from www. gov.uk/government/uploads. The NFER/DfE surveys on pupil behaviour are also available to download there.

Different levels of classroom behaviour

The education setting's behaviour policy is likely to clarify the nature and types of pupil behaviour that constitute low-level and high-level disruption. Table 5.1 provides a comprehensive list, which can act as an aide memoire for teachers.

Table 5.1

Low- and high-level behaviour disruptions

Low-level behaviour	High-level behaviour
Calling out	Swearing
Being off task	Destroying other pupils' work
Being out of seat in class	Making sexual/racial comments
Throwing and flicking objects or paper	Vandalising books and equipment
Distracting other pupils from their work	Violent, dangerous behaviour
Arriving late for lessons	Bullying
Being cheeky	Fighting
Talking when the teacher is talking	Walking out of class and school
Not listening to the teacher	Persistent lying
Forgetting to bring books/equipment	Bringing offensive weapons to school

Recording, analysing and tracking pupil behaviour

The **ABC analysis of behaviour** is a popular problem-solving approach used by teachers for recording and analysing significant pupil behaviour incidents. It also enables class and subject teachers to explore and understand the reasons why a pupil has misbehaved.

- **A** refers to **Antecedents** (i.e. the events leading up to the behaviour, or happening just before the behaviour occurs).
- **B** refers to the actual **Behaviour** that occurs.
- **C** refers to the **Consequences** (i.e. what happens after the behaviour incident occurs; how the pupil who misbehaved feels; how others (pupils and staff) react to the pupil's behaviour).

Figure 5.1 provides a model template for a teacher or TA to use to record a significant pupil behaviour incident, using the ABC approach.

Class and subject teachers may find it useful to support the ABC behaviour record by seeking the answers to the following reflective questions, which can help to inform the appropriate strategies to use to prevent the behaviour happening again.

- What appears to be the underlying cause of the pupil's misbehaviour?
- When and where (and how frequently) does the pupil display the behaviour?
- What are the triggers that set the pupil's misbehaviour off?
- What strategies could be used to help the pupil to change and manage their behaviour better?

Class and subject teachers may be requested by the SENCO or pastoral leader to track a pupil's behaviour across a day, or over five days. This helps to identify any 'hot spots', or where a pupil is experiencing barriers to their learning that result in them misbehaving as a coping strategy, to cover up for not being able to cope with the level of work (e.g. if it does not match their ability or reading age, or they cannot grasp a concept because the teacher has not delivered and explained it in the pupil's preferred learning style). Figure 5.2 provides a model template that teachers can use to track an individual's behaviour in each lesson, over a day.

The four Rs framework for effective behaviour management

The four Rs framework offers teachers a practical approach for consistently managing pupil behaviour. The four Rs represent **Rights**, **Rules**, **Routines** and **Responsibilities**. The framework not only supports an education setting's behaviour policy, but also helps to reinforce the classroom rules and code of conduct. Teachers will wish to check that TAs use the same consistent behaviour management approach in order to prevent pupils playing one member of staff off against another. Table 5.2 provides a useful summary of the features of the four Rs behaviour management framework, which can act as an aide memoire.

Pupil name: _____

Date and place of incident: _____

Antecedents:

Behaviour:

Consequences:

Figure 5.1 ABC template to record a significant pupil behaviour incident

Nature of the pupil's classroom behaviour	Lesson 1	Lesson 2	Lesson 3	Lesson 4

Pupil name: _____ Date: _____

Nature of the pupil's classroom behaviour (Tick the relevant box if the feature was present)	Lesson 1	Lesson 2	Lesson 3	Lesson 4
Arrived to the lesson on time	❏	❏	❏	❏
Arrived to the lesson late	❏	❏	❏	❏
Settled down quickly to work	❏	❏	❏	❏
Took some time to settle down to work	❏	❏	❏	❏
Brought the correct books and equipment to the lesson	❏	❏	❏	❏
Did not bring books or equipment required for the lesson	❏	❏	❏	❏
Worked well throughout the lesson	❏	❏	❏	❏
Wasted time in the lesson and was off task frequently	❏	❏	❏	❏
Completed all work in the lesson	❏	❏	❏	❏
Refused to do work in the lesson	❏	❏	❏	❏
Had to be moved away from other pupils in the lesson	❏	❏	❏	❏
Used unacceptable and abusive language in the lesson	❏	❏	❏	❏
Was aggressive in the lesson	❏	❏	❏	❏
Disrupted other pupils from getting on with their work	❏	❏	❏	❏
Got out of seat and wandered around the classroom	❏	❏	❏	❏
Left the classroom without permission	❏	❏	❏	❏
Refused to obey or follow the teacher's/TA's instructions	❏	❏	❏	❏
Ate in class without permission	❏	❏	❏	❏
Was rude to staff	❏	❏	❏	❏
Was rude to other pupils	❏	❏	❏	❏
Interfered with equipment and/or other pupils' work	❏	❏	❏	❏
Talked when the teacher was talking	❏	❏	❏	❏
Shouted out in class	❏	❏	❏	❏
Threw things around the classroom	❏	❏	❏	❏
Was unable to work co-operatively with other pupils	❏	❏	❏	❏

Figure 5.2 Individual pupil behaviour tracking sheet

Table 5.2

The four Rs behaviour management framework

Rights	Routines
The rights of all pupils in the class to: – learn; – be safe (physically and emotionally); – have dignity and respect. The right of every teacher/TA to: – teach and provide support for learning.	Daily routines must be followed consistently when: – entering and leaving the classroom; – getting work out and putting work away; – moving around the classroom; – asking and answering questions; – going to use the computer or visit the school library; – going into and out of a school assembly.
Rules	**Responsibilities**
There are three basic rules that all pupils must follow: 1. Follow the teacher's/TA's directions and instructions. 2. Keep hands, feet and objects to themselves. 3. No swearing, name-calling or put-downs.	Helping pupils to take greater responsibility for their own behaviour involves using the language of choice. For example: – 'If you choose not to settle down to your work, then you will be choosing to stay in at break/playtime to finish it.' – 'I need you to choose to put that magazine away and go back to your place.' – 'Thank you for choosing to sit away from Peter and to get on with your work.'

© 2015, *Special Educational Needs for Qualified and Trainee Teachers*, Rita Cheminais, Routledge.

Twenty top tips for managing pupil behaviour

Teachers, particularly those who are trainees and newly qualified, will find the following list of twenty top practical tips for managing pupil behaviour a useful point of reference. They are tried and tested and complement those produced as a checklist for teachers by Charlie Taylor, the government's expert adviser on behaviour in schools, which is illustrated in Figure 5.3.

1 Condemn the behaviour and not the pupil.

2 Reprimand the pupil privately rather than publicly.

3 Listen to the pupil's reason and explanation for their behaviour.

4 Deal with the behaviour calmly and quietly to minimise disruption.

5 Catch the pupil being well behaved and use positive praise to reinforce good behaviour.

6 Avoid confrontation and defuse it with humour or by changing the subject.

7 Refer the pupil regularly to the classroom rules, which are phrased positively.

8 Use non-verbal cues (e.g. a look, raised eyebrows, being silent, making eye contact, using symbols).

9 Give the pupil a job to do or a message to take.

10 Provide time out and a quiet area in the classroom where the pupil can cool off and calm down.

11 Teach the pupil to use anger management techniques (e.g. count to ten, squeeze a stress ball, do some deep breathing, 'sit' on their hands).

12 Ensure that tasks are matched to pupil ability and reading age.

13 Pair the pupil up with a peer who is a good role model for behaviour.

14 Make explicit to the pupil the consequences of their misbehaviour.

15 Apply sanctions for misbehaviour fairly and consistently.

16 Introduce breaks from task or vary tasks to prevent boredom, which can lead to misbehaviour (e.g. brain breaks and brain exercises).

17 Seat the pupil in front of the teacher at the front of the class.

18 Ensure that the pupil can succeed at something in the lesson or during the day.

19 Use the pupil's home–school diary to keep parents and carers informed about their child's behaviour – both positive and negative aspects.

20 When a pupil's behaviour is dangerous or may compromise the safety of other pupils in the class, move the pupil out of the classroom and call for a senior member of staff to deal with the pupil's behaviour.

Meeting Ofsted's expectations for pupil behaviour

When Ofsted inspectors evaluate behaviour and safety during inspection, they will consider:

● pupils' attitudes to learning and whether these help or hinder their progress in lessons (e.g. whether they are ready and eager to learn; how quickly they settle at the start of a lesson; whether they have the right equipment; their willingness to

Classroom

- Know the names and roles of any adults in class
- Meet and greet pupils when they enter the classroom
- Display rules in the class – and ensure that the pupils and staff know what they are
- Display the tariff of sanctions in class
- Have a system in place to follow through with all sanctions
- Display the tariff of rewards in class
- Have a system in place to follow through with all rewards
- Have a visual timetable on the wall
- Follow the school behaviour policy

Pupils

- Know the names of children
- Have a plan for children who are likely to misbehave
- Ensure other adults in the class know the plan
- Understand pupils' special needs

Teaching

- Ensure that all resources are prepared in advance
- Praise the behaviour you want to see more of
- Praise children doing the right things more than criticising those who are doing the wrong thing (parallel praise)
- Differentiate
- Stay calm
- Have clear routines for transitions and for stopping the class
- Teach children the class routines

Parents

- Give feedback to parents about their child's behaviour – let them know about the good days as well as the bad ones

Figure 5.3 Charlie Taylor's behaviour checklist for teachers

(Source: DfE 2011a: 5)

answer teachers' questions; whether they remain focused when working as part of the whole class, in a group or on their own; the tidiness of their work and the pride they show in its presentation; and the overall effort they make);

- pupils' behaviour around school and in lessons, including the extent of low-level disruption;

- pupils' attitudes and behaviour towards, and respect for, other peers and adults, and their freedom from bullying, harassment and discrimination;
- pupils' attendance and punctuality at school and in lessons;
- how well teachers manage the behaviour and expectations of pupils to ensure that all pupils have an equal and fair chance to thrive and learn in an atmosphere of respect and dignity;
- the extent to which the school ensures the systematic and consistent management of behaviour;
- whether pupils feel safe, and their ability to assess and manage risk appropriately and to keep themselves safe;
- whether teachers keep pupils safe (e.g. undertaking effective risk assessments, following e-safety arrangements and safeguarding procedures);
- the extent to which leaders and managers have created a positive ethos in the school;
- pupils' respect for the school's learning environment, facilities and equipment (e.g. not dropping litter) and whether they take pride in their appearance (e.g. wearing school uniform);
- the impact of strategies to improve pupils' behaviour and attendance.

Inspectors will wish to talk to pupils about behaviour, bullying and feeling safe in school, as well as looking at a sample of case studies, to check on the experiences of particular groups of pupils, including LAC and those with SEND and mental health needs.

Teachers and trainee teachers may find it useful to read the outstanding and good grade descriptors for behaviour and safety in the latest version of the Ofsted *School Inspection Handbook* (Ofsted 2014a), which can be accessed at www.ofsted.gov.uk.

Identifying and tackling bullying, including cyber-bullying

Bullying creates a barrier to children's learning and prevents them from learning effectively and feeling safe. Research shows that pupils with SEND are significantly more likely to be bullied or victimised than those without. Pupils with SEND are a target for bullying and experience personal distress because they:

- are perceived by some other peers as being 'different', and therefore an easy target for bullying;
- do not realise they are actually being bullied and therefore incidents go unreported;
- have limited communication skills and thus find it difficult to tell an adult that they are being bullied;
- are more isolated as a result of having fewer friends than other peers;
- forget to report a bullying incident immediately because of their poor memory skills;
- are sometimes dual-placement pupils spending time in a mainstream school for some part of the week, and therefore being more exposed to bullying from some of their mainstream peers.

The definition of bullying

Bullying is defined as behaviour by an individual or a group that is repeated over time and that intentionally hurts another individual or group, either physically or emotionally.

The Anti-Bullying Alliance's (ABA)'s pupil-friendly definition of bullying states 'people doing nasty or unkind things to you on purpose more than once, which it is difficult to stop' (ABA/CaF 2011: 2).

Cyber-bullying is the act of using the internet and other digital (mobile) technologies to upset or humiliate another person.

Pupils with SEND have the same rights and entitlements to be safe and free from bullying as all other children and young people, under the Equality Act 2010.

Cyber-bullying and pupils with SEND

Research has shown that pupils with SEND tend to be the victims of cyber-bullying owing to peer rejection, social isolation and social skills deficiencies. The internet and digital technology is a popular medium for pupils with SEND to use for social engagement, because they do not have to reveal their disability to others. Unfortunately, cyber-bullying can occur 24 hours a day over seven days a week, and much of it outside school hours.

Cyber-bullying ranges from threatening messages being sent via email, text or instant messaging (IM), having an email account hacked into, or having an online identity stolen. Some proficient cyber-bullies can also create a social media webpage to bully a victim. There is a gender difference in the type of cyber-bullying undertaken by boys and girls. For example, boys usually resort to 'sexting' or sending messages that threaten physical harm. Girls, on the other hand, prefer to spread lies and rumours, to expose their victim's secrets online or to exclude the victim from emails.

Cyber-bullying can cause many negative effects on victims, which include low self-esteem and feeling hurt, angry, helpless, isolated, depressed or even suicidal. Unfortunately cyber-bullying can be done anonymously, which results in the pupil with SEND not being sure who is targeting and taunting them.

The McAfee research report entitled *Digital Deception: The Online Behaviour of Teens*, published in January 2014, gave some alarming statistics about children and young people's access to, and use of, online and digital (mobile) technology. Some of the headline statistics are:

- 53 per cent of children and young people go online without the supervision of parents or carers.
- 66 per cent of children and young people use a smartphone for internet access.
- 26 per cent of children and young people spend between four and six hours or more online every day.
- 22 per cent of children and young people have witnessed the cyber-bullying of a friend or classmate.
- 16 per cent of children and young people have been victims of cyber-bullying.
- 10 per cent of teenagers have been approached online by an adult they do not know.

- Only 19 per cent of parents and carers have installed parental controls on computers and other mobile devices that their child accesses.
- Between 31 and 35 per cent of children and young people have posted their email address or a photograph of themselves online, or have given an online description of what they look like.

How to identify if a pupil is experiencing cyber-bullying

Teachers and trainee teachers should look out for the following signs of the effects of cyber-bullying on a pupil with SEND:

- becoming sad, angry or distressed during or after using the internet or a mobile phone;
- appearing anxious when receiving an email, text, instant message or email;
- avoiding discussion of and being secretive about their computer or mobile phone activities;
- withdrawing from family, friends and activities that they previously enjoyed;
- a decline in the output and completion of school work;
- beginning to be reluctant to go to school and being absent on occasions;
- showing changes in mood and behaviour (e.g. disturbed sleep patterns; loss of appetite; appearing anxious, depressed or suicidal).

Top tips for internet and digital technology safety

The following top tips are useful for teachers and trainee teachers to follow:

- Do not allow pupils to respond to any text messages, emails or other online posts that are negative or hurtful about them.
- Keep all the evidence of cyber-bullying incidents and report any inappropriate sexual images that pupils have received to the headteacher, who must then refer this on to the police, as it is a child protection issue.
- Show pupils a YouTube or video clip on the dangers of cyber-bullying and the consequences for perpetrators.
- Keep reinforcing online/digital safety with pupils (e.g. posters with rules and reminders about never sharing their passwords or posting any personal details online, or meeting unknown people encountered online).
- Ensure that parental controls are installed on smartphones and tablets as well as computers, to filter any inappropriate web content.
- Set limits and boundaries for internet and iPad use in lessons.
- Teach pupils with SEND how to create safe and strong passwords for log-ins.

Teachers and trainees will find the following websites helpful on bullying and cyber-bullying:

- www.kidscape.org.uk/cyberbullying;
- www.beatbullying.org;
- www.childline.org.uk;

- www.antibullyingalliance.org.uk;
- www.thinkuknow.co.uk, which is a Child Exploitation and Online Protection Centre (CEOP) programme providing a range of free resources.

The ABA and Contact a Family (CaF) offer a free resource for teachers entitled *Cyberbullying and Children and Young People with SEN and Disabilities: Guidance for Teachers and Other Professionals* (2012), which can be downloaded from www.antibullyingalliance.org.uk.

The DfE has a useful publication relating to bullying and SEND available at www.gov.uk entitled *Preventing and Tackling Bullying: Advice for Headteachers, Staff and Governing Bodies* (2013e). There are also two excellent video resources worth viewing: *Make Them Go Away*, which features bullying involving children with disabilities (https://www.youtube.com/watch?v=Cw0VrC5ODKA), and *Let's Fight It Together*, which focuses on cyber-bullying (www.childnet.com/resources/lets-fight-it-together).

Identifying and tackling low self-esteem

The concept, causes and characteristics of pupils with low self-esteem

Self-esteem refers to the way in which individuals see, think and feel about themselves or judge their self-worth. It is also about how they think others feel about them or perceive them. Low self-esteem negatively affects pupils' capacity to learn. Low self-esteem is often evident in pupils with social, mental and emotional health needs.

Low self-esteem in pupils may be a result of their:

- feeling that they do not fit in with their peer group or live up to media images of how children and young people should be;
- need to adjust to adolescence;
- striving for independence from their parents or carers in front of their peers and friends;
- worrying that they do not have the right skills for undertaking an activity;
- feeling they can never live up to the expectations of their parents, carers or others.

Teachers and trainee teachers need to look out for the characteristics of low self-esteem in vulnerable pupils:

- having difficulty expressing themselves;
- fearing rejection by friends and family;
- being reluctant to complete work for fear of failure;
- telling lies to mask their feelings;
- going on the defensive to hide their weaknesses;
- blaming others for their failings;
- seeking constant reassurance from teachers and other supportive adults.

Positive approaches to raising pupils' self-esteem

Teachers and trainee teachers should find the following approaches useful in helping to raise pupils' self-esteem, particularly of those who have a poor self-image:

- Encourage pupils to adopt a 'can-do' approach.
- Give praise and recognition to counter pupils' negative feelings.
- Give pupils responsibilities to make them feel valued.
- Focus on pupils' strengths and talents.
- Offer reassurance and encouragement.
- Build success into every day for pupils.
- Act as a positive role model for good self-esteem.
- Show pupils that you can sometimes make mistakes.
- Use positive affirmations and language.
- Ensure that peers show respect for pupils' thoughts and efforts.
- Teach pupils to cope with disappointments or failures.
- Prepare pupils for new experiences or changes in routines.
- Help pupils to set themselves goals or targets to make them feel better about themselves.

Developing a safe and emotionally intelligent learning environment

The definition of emotional intelligence

Emotional intelligence is the ability to recognise, understand, manage and appropriately express emotions. It is about managing yourself and your emotions and understanding and interpreting the emotions and feelings of others.

Developing emotional intelligence among pupils within the classroom is important because emotions influence motivation, concentration, creativity, behaviour, learning, memory and achievement. Knowing how to interpret and manage emotions also contributes to pupils' well-being.

Emotional intelligence influences pupils' self-esteem. If pupils feel good about themselves, then they will learn more efficiently, and be happier and more cooperative. A pupil who is angry or anxious will not learn as effectively.

Strategies for developing pupils' emotional intelligence

When the teacher or trainee teacher understands pupils' feelings, good adult–pupil relationships become easier to establish. Teachers and trainee teachers can develop pupils' emotional intelligence by:

- creating situations involving successful social interactions to help to build pupils' self-esteem and develop their positive thinking;
- designing activities where pupils have to work together cooperatively, and debriefing them on the nature of the cooperative skills they have used;

- modelling effective social behaviour for pupils and encouraging them to talk about this and how they might feel in hypothetical situations;
- using social stories to help pupils to develop an understanding about feelings and emotions;
- encouraging pupils to talk through on a one-to-one basis with you why something is bothering them;
- listening with empathy to understand how pupils are feeling;
- articulating your feelings within the classroom;
- asking pupils to share their feelings about a subject or topic;
- allowing pupils to put their feelings on Post-it notes and post them in a box in the classroom anonymously if they are unwilling to share feelings openly;
- using role play and drama activities to enable pupils to express their emotions and feelings;
- incorporating circle time into the weekly class routine to give pupils the opportunity to explore feelings and share emotions together in a safe and emotionally literate environment.

Further useful resources

The following resources offer a valuable point of reference for qualified and trainee teachers.

Of the DfE's Advanced training materials for teaching pupils with SEND, two modules will be of particular interest:

1 Autism Spectrum Disorders (ASD);

2 Behavioural, Emotional and Social Difficulties (BESD).

These multi-media resources can be accessed at www.advanced-training.org.uk/.

The IDP offers an excellent range of interactive multi-media training resources for teachers and trainee teachers, which are organised by the phase of education and the nature of SEND. Two modules in particular will be useful in relation to topics covered in this chapter:

1 Supporting Children with Behavioural, Emotional and Social Difficulties;

2 Supporting Children on the Autism Spectrum.

These can be accessed at www.idponline.org.uk/.

There are useful reasonably priced photocopiable resources produced by Rob Long, who is an experienced expert in the field of behaviour, available from www.roblong. co.uk. Of particular interest are the following resources:

- *Classroom Survival Skills* (Long 2000a);
- *Supporting Troubled Children* (Long 2000b);
- *Making Sense of Teenagers* (Long 2000c).

Questions for reflection

1 In response to the DfE's updated advice on teachers' powers to discipline pupils, what are your views on this aspect? Describe the approaches that you find work best to tackle low-level disruption from pupils.

2 A pupil with ADHD in your class is becoming more disruptive. They distract other peers when working, they walk around the classroom and they make rude remarks about the work set. How will you deal with this situation?

3 After viewing and using the IDP or the DfE's Advanced training modules on ASD or BESD, identify your own new learning on either of these topics and describe how you will apply what you have learnt to your own classroom context.

4 A pupil with SEND in one of your classes has recently become withdrawn, is absent on the same day each week and is reluctant to use the computer in lessons. You suspect they may be a victim of bullying/cyber-bullying. Describe the steps you will take to explore and address this issue.

Fulfilling wider professional development responsibilities

This chapter covers:

- Developing effective teamwork with other colleagues
- Productive partnerships with multi-agency practitioners
- Working in partnership with the SENCO
- The person-centred approach
- Coaching and mentoring to build teacher capacity in SEND
- Deploying TAs effectively
- Effective partnership working with parents and carers of pupils with SEND

Developing effective teamwork with other colleagues

Teachers usually belong to more than one team in an education setting. For example, they may belong to a curriculum team and also to a Key Stage team. Teachers usually join together in these groups in order to share strategies, best practice and concerns, as well as to celebrate successes.

The acronym TEAM refers to the principle that 'together each achieves more', in an effort to prevent one person trying to do everything themselves. The term 'team' is defined as being three or more people working together towards the same goal. Teams exist in order to get things done. How well they achieve their goal is dependent upon on how well members of the team work together.

The benefits of teamwork

There are a number of benefits of teachers working together as part of a team. These include:

- preventing work overload by distributing tasks fairly and equitably among others;
- enhancing open and free communication between teachers;
- strengthening commitment;
- giving greater ownership in decision making;

- enhancing professional learning opportunities through the sharing of knowledge;
- creating a sense of belonging through collegiality;
- increasing openness, honesty and trust among members of the team;
- raising teacher morale in knowing there are other colleagues to rely on for support.

Characteristics of effective teams

A number of key characteristics can be identified in effective strong teams. These include the following:

- There is a genuine willingness to work together and to share ideas, knowledge and resources.
- The strengths and talents of team members are acknowledged and used.
- Creativity is allowed and encouraged.
- There is a good level of care, support and feedback given to each other.
- There is genuine and sincere respect and confidence among team members.
- There is dedication to the common cause or goals, with regular feedback on work in progress.
- All team members are clear about the expectations of each other.

While the success of any team is dependent on it having a strong and effective leader, different team members are likely to exhibit different strengths and roles. For example:

- **Leader** – creates a common purpose and vision for the work of the team; clarifies the objectives; ensures that all team members are motivated, committed and involved; coordinates the team's work and checks on its progress.
- **Thinker** – collects and analyses information; listens to what other team members have to say; watches what goes on; thinks before they contribute their own ideas; anticipates and thinks through problems, and sees solutions.
- **Achiever** – is eager for the team to succeed and achieve results; wants to progress towards goals quickly; becomes impatient with delays; challenges assumptions; proposes improvements; is enthusiastic; questions complacency.
- **Carer** – is concerned that everybody is fitting in; builds bridges around the team; contributes humour; works to develop and foster a strong team spirit; is keen to get team members to agree; watches out for feelings and attitudes; eases any tensions.
- **Doer** – always wants to be active; is prepared to get involved to help others; wants to see progress and adherence to plans; gets bored with too much discussion and not enough action; dislikes time wasting; works hard to finish and complete the task set.

Teachers may wish to reflect on which role they play in any team that they belong to in the education setting.

The checklist in Figure 6.1 will help to identify how well the teams you belong to are working together effectively, and which aspects of teamwork require further development or improvement.

Teamwork aspect	Teamwork activities	✓ Yes or ✗ No	Comments
Communication	Communication is regular between team members so all know what is going on. Team members' views and ideas are listened to. All team members are clear about what the team's overall goal and objectives are.		
Coordination	All team members are clear about their own role in the team. All team members are clear about each other's roles and tasks. Everyone in the team is clear about what has to be done and by when.		
Workload	Workload in the team is allocated fairly. When one of the team is under pressure, others in the team offer to help out. There is agreement among all team members as to how team tasks should be shared out.		
Feedback	The contributions and efforts of all team members are valued and acknowledged. Team members are committed to helping each other learn. Team members are able to accept constructive criticism.		
Effort	Everyone in the team is doing their fair share and is contributing equally.		
Cohesion	All team members work together to achieve the same goal. The team remains united even when there may be some disagreement.		

Figure 6.1 Teamwork checklist

Code of conduct for productive teamwork

- Help each other to be right rather than wrong.
- Look for ways to make new ideas work rather than seek reasons for why they will not work.
- If you are not sure about something, check it out rather than dismiss it.
- Help each other to succeed in the team.
- Speak positively about other team members.
- Keep a positive team attitude to succeed against all odds.
- Stick to the team agenda and plan, and avoid going off at a tangent.
- Be enthusiastic about the team's work and efforts.
- Believe in what you are doing and persevere when the going gets tough.
- Have fun and enjoy the teamwork experience.

Productive partnerships with multi-agency practitioners

The draft 2014 *SEND Code of Practice* identifies that children and young people with SEND need integrated, well-coordinated and coherent support from education, health and social care services in order to help them to achieve their agreed outcomes. Through collaborative working, these frontline multi-agency practitioners can achieve far more for pupils with SEND than they could if they worked separately, in isolation from each other. The LA's 'local offer' sets out the range of different services available locally to children with SEND, as well as the support that children, young people and their families can access outside the local area. It also gives information on how these services can be accessed.

The concept of multi-agency partnership working is where frontline practitioners from more than one agency work together jointly, sharing aims, information, tasks and responsibilities, in order to intervene early and respond promptly to the changing needs of children and young people.

Pupils with SEND who have an EHC plan are likely to have practitioners from health and social care services working directly with them in or beyond the education setting (e.g. an occupational therapist or physiotherapist, a speech and language therapist, a CAMHS worker, a social worker or counsellor, or an outreach teacher from the local autism team). The main purpose of all of the frontline practitioners is to help to remove or minimise barriers to learning and participation for pupils with SEND. In addition, through their interventions, the practitioners aim to contribute to improving the well-being and academic outcomes for pupils with SEND. The overall contributions that multi-agency practitioners make should also add value to the work of the education setting, where pupils with SEND are educated. Table 6.1 provides an overview of the roles of different multi-agency practitioners.

The SEND pupil's EHC plan will specify the exact nature of the provision from health and social care services that will complement the special educational provision being delivered. The focus on outcomes from all of these services, which may include provision from the voluntary community sector, ensures that each practitioner is clear about what is expected of them. When reviewing the EHC plan with parents or carers, the pupil themselves, the SENCO and any external professionals who are requested

Table 6.1

The role of external multi-agency practitioners working with pupils with SEND

Education Welfare Officer	Social Care Worker	School Nurse	Educational Psychologist
– supports schools in improving pupils' attendance; – undertakes targeted individual and group case work; – protects children from the risks of exploitation and harm; – monitors the licensing of local child employment and child entertainment; – involved in school-based attendance projects; – liaises with Home Education and Out-of-School Learning Services; – provides professional advice and support to schools on safeguarding; – supports and advises parents and carers to ensure they fulfil their statutory responsibilities with respect to the education of their children; – involved in court action – parent/carer prosecutions for their child's school non-attendance.	– undertakes rapid response case work; – supports the CaF process; – supports the school's personal, social and health education (PSHE) programme; – signposts to specialist services; – provides counselling and mentoring to pupils and families; – builds relationships between schools and families; – provides pupil support for bereavement, self-esteem, behaviour and attendance, depression, self-harming, school anxiety/phobia, family violence, substance abuse, bullying and suicidal threats; – acts as an advocate for children, young people and their families; – helps to identify school staff and other agency practitioners who can help to maximise pupil success.	– provides confidential advice and guidance on a range of health-related issues including nutrition, exercise, smoking, mental health, drug abuse and sexual health; – promotes good physical, emotional and mental health, and supports children and young people to make healthy life choices; – contributes to the school's PSHE programme and the Healthy Schools initiative; – helps to develop and update the school's health and safety policy and the sex education policy; – provides advice on healthy eating; – contributes to the school's extended services provision by running a drop-in clinic for children, young people and their parents/carers on or near the school site; – supports individual pupils with long-term medical needs who have health plans; – provides immunisation to pupils, where appropriate; – runs parent/carer groups.	– undertakes early identification of problems and early intervention; – engages in action research to promote increased teacher knowledge of good inclusive practice and raise expectations; – engages in projects to raise pupil achievement and improve provision for BESD pupils; – supports the professional development of teachers and TAs, and contributes to governor training; – works collaboratively with other multi-agency practitioners; – supports parents and carers as key partners in their child's learning and well-being; – promotes a solution-oriented approach to problem solving in relation to pupil learning, behaviour and well-being; – works with individual children and young people who have severe, complex and challenging needs; – involved in the statutory assessment of children with the most complex needs.

Play Therapist	Speech & Language Therapist	Careers Adviser	ASD Outreach Teacher
– helps children through the medium of play to understand the issues that are preventing them from living a happy life; – offers children coping strategies to enable them to manage their feelings such as anger, fear, anxiety, depression and conflict; – helps children to relax and enjoy the play experience; – builds up a relationship of trust with children to enable them to talk about their feelings with ease; – undertakes assessment and observation of children at school and home to identify needs; – works in partnership with parents and carers and other practitioners to advise them on how best to support and meet children's needs through play and to build up their resilience.	– assesses children's communication needs; – provides direct specialist speech therapy sessions to individual and small groups of children; – provides training to teachers and support assistants in delivering speech and language programmes; – contributes to whole-school in-service training on SLCN; – advises on resources, ICT and communication aids; – helps teachers and TAs to differentiate the curriculum; – liaises with parents and carers on how they can help to support and promote their children's SLCN at home; – monitors and evaluates the impact of speech and language programmes delivered to pupils; – works collaboratively with other professionals such as the Educational Psychologist, School Nurse and Occupational Therapist.	– provides one-to-one support, advice and guidance to pupils aged 13–19 on careers, training and employment opportunities; – acts as an advocate and mediator for young people, particularly those with SEND or who are vulnerable; – works in partnership with other agencies such as FE colleges, Youth Service, Social Services, Health Services, Housing, employers and training providers and the voluntary sector; – helps young people to access volunteering, community activities and sport; – works with parents and carers to enable them to support their children's career aspirations; – accesses community support from the arts, study support and other guidance networks in the local area, particularly in finding work experience placements.	– provides advice and support on assessing pupils' needs; – provides direct teaching to individual and small groups of ASD pupils, following specific programmes; – undertakes observations on ASD pupils and feeds back to teachers and TAs; – advises on appropriate resources and strategies to address the triad of impairment; – gives demonstration lessons; – advises on personalised learning approaches and curriculum modifications; – contributes to whole-school in-service staff training on the autism spectrum; – advises teachers and SENCOs on specific interventions and programmes for pupils with ASD; – provides feedback on the progress of pupils with ASD in their specific intervention programmes; – liaises with other practitioners and colleagues; – liaises with the parents and carers of pupils with ASD and keeps them informed of progress in intervention programmes.

(continued)

Table 6.1 (continued)

The role of external multi-agency practitioners working with pupils with SEND

Specialist Outreach Teacher for Sensory Impairment (HI/VI)	Primary Mental Health Worker (CAMHS)	Occupational Therapist	Physiotherapist
– undertakes any specialist teaching; – provides practical advice on how to minimise barriers to learning and enhance curriculum access; – advises on the provision of any specialist equipment, resources or aids to support hearing and vision; – models good practice in meeting the needs of children and young people with sensory impairments; – advises on any special access arrangements for statutory tests and external examinations; – contributes advice to a child or young person's SEND statutory assessment; – provides INSET and bespoke training to staff in schools and children's centres on how to remove barriers to learning and participation; – offers advice to parents and carers on home adaptations and signposts them to further information.	– undertakes assessments to identify children's mental health problems; – promotes positive emotional health and well-being by providing drop-in sessions, workshops, advice and information to parents and carers, school and children's centre staff, children and young people on building resilience; – advises on referral and facilitates access to specialist CAMHS provision as appropriate; – liaises and collaborates with other multi-agency professionals, teachers and support staff; – offers direct inputs and short-term interventions with individual and small groups of children; – provides INSET and bespoke training; – supports the implementation of Family Social, Emotional Aspects of Learning (SEAL), targeted mental health programmes, Healthy Schools and Healthy FE framework.	– undertakes assessments and observations of children to identify the level of difficulties and needs; – provides direct interventions to children and young people who experience difficulties with their practical and social daily living skills; – identifies and puts in place appropriate strategies to remove barriers to learning and participation; – provides advice and training for parents and carers and for children's workforce practitioners on how best to work with and support children and young people; – provides programmes of work and interventions delivered by themselves or through others; – offers advice on the type of specialist equipment to use and the modifications to make to the classroom or at home.	– undertakes assessment of children's or young people's movement difficulties; – provides direct therapy, physical interventions, advice and support to minimise barriers to learning and participation; – works in partnership and liaises with other children's workforce practitioners to meet the needs of children and young people; – provides training and advice for parents and carers and for children's workforce practitioners on how best to meet children's or young people's needs; – provides programmes of work and practical strategies to support children and young people in different environments; – advises on specialist equipment and appliances; – supports special therapeutic swimming and hydrotherapy.

Behaviour Support Teacher	Community Police Officer	Family Support Worker	Parent Partnership Adviser
– undertakes assessments to identify pupils' emotional and behavioural difficulties;	– supports schools in reducing truancy and exclusions;	– identifies the needs of vulnerable families under stress;	– listens to the concerns of parents and carers;
– provides direct support and interventions to enable pupils to manage their behaviour and feelings;	– helps to reduce victimisation, criminality and anti-social behaviour within schools and local communities;	– offers practical help and advice to families experiencing problems;	– offers home visits;
– provides advice, guidance and support to staff in schools on how to manage pupils' behaviour;	– helps to identify and work with pupils at risk of becoming victims of crime and bullying, or becoming young offenders;	– helps parents and carers to enhance their home management and parenting skills;	– offers confidential and impartial advice and information on SEND and SEND legislation/Codes of Practice;
– assists staff in schools to deliver relevant programmes and interventions;	– supports school staff in dealing with incidents of crime, victimisation or anti-social behaviour;	– delivers parent and carer workshops and parenting programmes on a range of topics;	– supports parents and carers in meetings;
– advises on target setting and behaviour plans for pupils with BESD;	– promotes the participation of pupils in the life of schools and in the wider community, (e.g. volunteering and youth activities, community projects);	– assists Social Care Workers in assessing families' needs;	– delivers workshops and holds drop-in sessions at the one-stop shop or other local venues on a variety of relevant SEND topics;
– provides advice and guidance to parents and carers on how to support their children's behaviour at home;	– provides educational inputs for pupils in the classroom on aspects of citizenship and personal safety as part of PSHE;	– provides direct short-term emergency care in the family home;	– provides information about disagreement arrangements and the Special Educational Needs and Disability Tribunal (SENDIST);
– liaises with other multi-agency professionals;	– works in partnership with other agencies such as the Youth Offending Team (YOT), Youth Justice and Connexions;	– attends case conferences, team around the child (TAC) meetings, team around the family (TAF) meetings, EHC plan review meetings and any court case hearings;	– supports parents and carers in communicating their concerns and views on specific SEND issues to schools;
– signposts to further information, support and services;	– builds positive relationships between the police and young people.	– liaises and works in partnership with other multi-agency practitioners;	– supports parents and carers of children with SEND to put their views in writing and to understand any letters, reports or documents they receive from the local authority, multi-agency professionals or school.
– delivers INSET, bespoke training and workshops to school staff, parents and carers.		– helps parents and carers to access relevant education, training and employment;	
		– signposts parents and carers to other information, guidance and agencies.	

to attend, class and subject teachers will gain greater insight into how the additional interventions from the multi-agency services have made a positive difference. Where a pupil on SEN Support makes little or no progress over a sustained period of time, or continues to work at levels substantially below those expected of their peers of the same age, despite well-founded SEN Support having been put in place, the involvement of specialist practitioners/professionals from education, health and social care services should be sought. The SENCO and class teacher, together with the specialists, consider a range of well-founded and effective teaching approaches, appropriate equipment, strategies and interventions to further support the pupil's progress. The existing support is adapted or replaced according to how effective it has been in achieving the expected outcomes. The SENCO in the education setting will ensure that class and subject teachers are kept up to date with any changes in provision from specialist external services. This, in turn, will enable class and subject teachers to make any reasonable adjustments to the delivery of the curriculum, to the physical learning environment or to how information is delivered to pupils with SEND, who have more complex needs. Some of these pupils may need to make use of auxiliary aids in lessons (e.g. hearing loop, lapel microphones, visualisers, voice-activated computer software).

Good practice principles for working with multi-agency practitioners

In order to ensure that work in collaborative partnership with multi-agency practitioners is effective, it is useful for teachers and trainee teachers to follow ten key principles:

1 Know the roles of the multi-agency practitioners who work directly with pupils with SEND.

2 Ensure that multi-agency practitioners are clear about your role.

3 Understand the law and frameworks relating to SEND and medical needs.

4 Know the procedures and protocols for making a service referral, obtaining an assessment, seeking advice and securing further specialist interventions for pupils.

5 Use the correct channels of communication for information sharing and be aware of confidentiality issues.

6 Understand the professional language and terminology used by multi-agency practitioners.

7 Have realistic expectations about what can be achieved through collaborative partnership in a given timescale.

8 Respect and value equally the contributions of other practitioners who work with pupils with SEND.

9 Make time to meet with multi-agency practitioners to discuss and review the impact of interventions for targeted pupils with SEND (e.g. at or before the EHC plan review).

10 Know who to refer to in the education setting if you have any queries or issues about any aspect of the multi-agency provision being delivered.

A quick self-evaluation on the effectiveness of multi-agency partnerships

As part of a SEND pupil's EHC plan review, discussion focuses on the effectiveness of the additional interventions provided by education, health and social care services. The following questions offer class and subject teachers a framework for reviewing the impact and effectiveness of multi–agency provision.

- What has worked well in the provision from education, health and social care services?

- Why do you think it has worked well?

- What has not worked as well?

- What are the views from service users, parents or carers, and the practitioners themselves on why it has worked less well?

- What could be done to promote, facilitate and drive better integrated partnership working?

- How do we know that the multi–agency provision has made a difference?

Working in partnership with the SENCO

Every education setting must have a qualified teacher who takes on the role of the SENCO. Those new to the role have to undertake the National Award for Special Educational Needs Coordination training.

The SEND Regulations accompanying the Children and Families Act 2014 and the draft 2014 *SEND Code of Practice* outline clearly the role of the SENCO. This includes:

- determining the strategic development of SEND policy and provision in the education setting, with the headteacher and governing body;

- providing professional guidance to colleagues;

- overseeing the daily operation of the education setting's SEND policy;

- coordinating provision for pupils with SEND;

- liaising with the relevant designated teacher, where an LAC has SEND;

- advising on a graduated approach to providing SEN Support;

- advising on the deployment of the education setting's budget for SEND, and other resources to meet pupils' needs effectively;

- liaising with parents and carers of pupils with SEND;

- liaising with early years providers, other schools, educational psychologists, health and social care professionals, and independent or voluntary bodies;

- being a key point of contact with external agencies, especially the LA and their support services;

- liaising with the next phase of education, to ensure that pupils with SEND and their parents and carers are informed about options, and a smooth transition is planned;

- being aware of the provision in the LA 'local offer' to ensure that pupils with SEND and their families receive appropriate support;

- ensuring that, under the Equality Act 2010, 'reasonable adjustments' and access arrangements are made for pupils with SEND.

Class and subject teachers both need to work in partnership with the SENCO when they are identifying, assessing, reviewing and meeting the needs of pupils with SEND, whether they are on School Support or have an EHC plan. The SENCO will advise and guide teachers on how best to deliver high-quality personalised teaching, and on differentiating the curriculum appropriately, in order to maximise access and to meet a diversity of high-incidence SEND.

Working in partnership with the SENCO is crucial for all teachers as they familiarise themselves with the new SEND system, effective from 1 September 2014.

A good example of partnership working between the SENCO and a class teacher is in relation to using the person-centred approach as part of the annual EHC plan review process.

The person-centred approach

The definition of the person-centred approach

The person-centred approach:

- is a process of continual listening and learning, by focusing on what is important to the pupil with SEND now and in the future, and acting on this information, in partnership with their family and friends;
- encourages the participation of the pupil with SEND and their parents or carers, in a less formal way, in the EHC plan review process;
- takes into account the pupil's wishes and aspirations, the outcomes they seek and the support they need to achieve them;
- enables the pupil with SEND to identify:
  - what is working well and therefore should stay the same in their additional provision;
  - what is not working in the provision and therefore needs to change;
  - what really matters and is important to them and to their family and others;
  - how each person and professional who cares about them can help them to achieve their goals and aspirations (i.e. the support and help they need).

The features of the person-centred approach

- **The pupil with SEND is at the centre** – they choose who to invite to their review meeting and the venue and date for the meeting.
- **Family members and friends are partners in planning** – they add richness of detail to the SEND pupil's story, while providing possible clues for change in provision.
- **The plan reflects what is important** – to the pupil with SEND, their capacities and what support they require (i.e. what they can do, their talents and strengths and what is important to them).

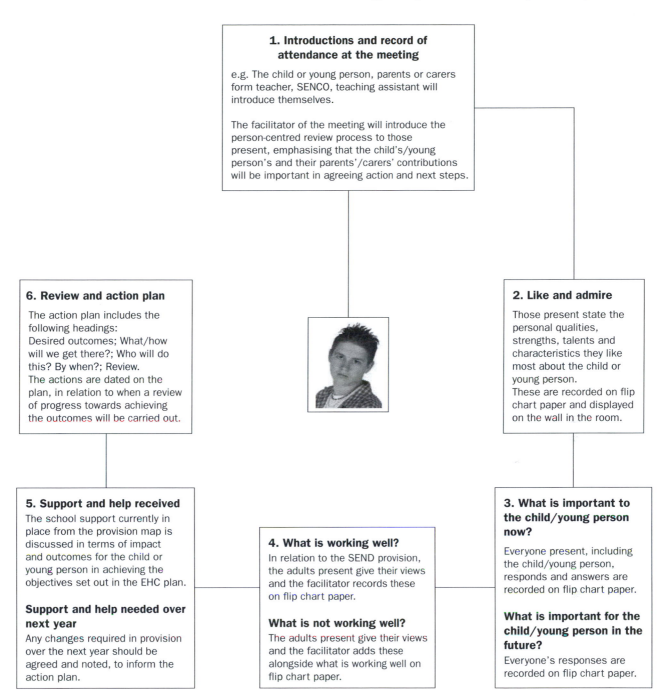

1. Introductions and record of attendance at the meeting

e.g. The child or young person, parents or carers form teacher, SENCO, teaching assistant will introduce themselves.

The facilitator of the meeting will introduce the person-centred review process to those present, emphasising that the child's/young person's and their parents'/carers' contributions will be important in agreeing action and next steps.

6. Review and action plan

The action plan includes the following headings:
Desired outcomes; What/how will we get there?; Who will do this? By when?; Review.
The actions are dated on the plan, in relation to when a review of progress towards achieving the outcomes will be carried out.

2. Like and admire

Those present state the personal qualities, strengths, talents and characteristics they like most about the child or young person.
These are recorded on flip chart paper and displayed on the wall in the room.

5. Support and help received

The school support currently in place from the provision map is discussed in terms of impact and outcomes for the child or young person in achieving the objectives set out in the EHC plan.

Support and help needed over next year

Any changes required in provision over the next year should be agreed and noted, to inform the action plan.

4. What is working well?

In relation to the SEND provision, the adults present give their views and the facilitator records these on flip chart paper.

What is not working well?

The adults present give their views and the facilitator adds these alongside what is working well on flip chart paper.

3. What is important to the child/young person now?

Everyone present, including the child/young person, responds and answers are recorded on flip chart paper.

What is important for the child/young person in the future?

Everyone's responses are recorded on flip chart paper.

Figure 6.2 Overview of the person-centred review process

- **The plan results in actions** – what is possible now and in later life (e.g. to feel included in school, in the community and, later, when working).

- **The plan results in ongoing listening, learning and further action** – learning through shared action to create change for the better in the SEND pupil's life.

The person-centred approach, like the structured conversation, is an empowering approach to use with parents or carers and their child, as it gives both ownership of the EHC planning and review process. Figure 6.2 explains the component parts of a person-centred review and Figure 6.3 provides a template for the review.

This review meeting belongs to

_____

I wish to invite to the meeting:

- _____

- _____

- _____

- _____

- _____

- _____

I want the meeting to be held at

_____

on the _____

_____

What has worked best for me

_____

_____

What has not gone so well for me

_____

_____

What I want to talk about at the meeting is:

- _____

- _____

- _____

- _____

- _____

What difference has the extra help made

_____

_____

What I want to happen next

_____

_____

Figure 6.3 Person-centred review meeting template

Coaching and mentoring to build teacher capacity in SEND

The SENCO may take on either a coaching or mentoring role with teachers to support them in improving an aspect of their practice in SEND, as well as enabling them to take the lead in the review process at SEN Support and/or at the EHC plan stage.

Coaching

The definition of coaching

Coaching is a structured sustained process for enabling the development of a specific aspect of a professional learner's (coachee's) practice. It does not tell the coachee what to do, but helps them to find their own solutions to workplace challenges. It involves helping the coachee to identify new ways of improving their performance. Coaching encourages the coachee to reflect on their practice and to see the big picture.

Types and styles of coaching

- **Informal coaching conversations** – a school leader or leading teacher uses coaching principles during short informal conversations about an issue raised by a colleague. It models a professional learning dialogue and supports the development of reflective thinking and practice.

- **Specialist coaching** – this uses specialist knowledge with a coachee to develop their practice in a specific area (e.g. SEND, or in a subject specialism or pedagogy). The coach will also have effective practice in coaching skills, qualities and principles.

- **Collaborative peer co-coaching** – partner teachers provide non-judgemental support to each other based on evidence from their own practice. Co-coaches each take on the role of coach and coachee.

- **Team coaching** – this is usually led by an external specialist coach or an internal experienced coach, and is focused on improvement in pedagogy or a particular subject/aspect (e.g. SEND) or a phase (primary or secondary).

- **Expert coaching** – this entails an expert external coach or a leading teacher working to develop coaching skills across the school.

- **Self-coaching** – this involves coaching principles and protocols being used by an individual on issues of professional concern to them.

- **Pupil coaching** – this is the promotion of pupil-to-pupil coaching, led by skilled teacher coaches within the school.

Mentoring

The definition of mentoring

Mentoring is a process used for supporting teachers, as professional learners, through significant career transitions (e.g. from ITT to NQT status, and from NQT through to a more confident and experienced teacher of pupils with SEND).

The SENCO as mentor

The SENCO is most likely to act as a SEND mentor for induction to an NQT, or to member of staff joining their team or department who is new to the school. A mentoring partnership is a very rewarding and enriching experience in terms of helping others to develop professionally and become more effective in their job.

What mentoring involves

Mentoring involves the SENCO as a mentor in the following activities:

- identifying learning goals and supporting the mentee's progression;
- increasing the mentee's control over their learning;
- active listening;
- modelling good practice in the inclusion of pupils with SEND, and articulating and discussing practice to raise awareness;
- observing the mentee teaching;
- engaging in shared learning experiences (e.g. team teaching, lesson observation, watching video clips of lessons);
- providing guidance, feedback and direction to the mentee;
- reviewing the mentee's progress and supporting action planning;
- contributing to the assessment and appraisal of the mentee;
- brokering access to further professional development opportunities (e.g. visiting other schools, including a special school).

At the end of the mentor–mentee relationship, the SENCO as mentor to an NQT, for example, may ask the mentee to reflect on the following questions:

- How do you feel the year has gone in relation to teaching pupils with SEND?
- What do you consider have been your most significant achievements in SEND this year?
- Which (if any) aspects of your work teaching pupils with SEND have you found most challenging?
- Which aspects of your work with SEND pupils would you wish to develop further?

Deploying TAs effectively

The effective deployment of TAs is crucial in relation to having the maximum impact on the progress of the pupils they support and work with. There has been extensive research in recent years that has explored TA deployment, training and effectiveness. Some of the key findings from this research are highlighted below.

In 2010, Ofsted published their *Special Educational Needs and Disability Review*, which found that:

> Where additional adult support was provided in the classroom for individuals, this was sometimes a barrier to including them successfully and enabling them to participate. . . . When a child or young person was supported closely by an adult, the adult focused on the completion of the task rather than on the actual

learning. Adults intervened too quickly, so preventing children and young people from having time to think or to learn from their mistakes.

(Ofsted 2010: 46, para. 99)

In the 2011 White Paper *Support and Aspiration: A New Approach to Special Educational Needs and Disability*, the DfE remarked:

Within schools, support staff can make a real difference to the achievement of pupils with SEN, but they need to be deployed and used effectively in order to do so. However, teaching assistant time should never be a substitute for teaching from a qualified teacher. Too often the most vulnerable pupils are supported almost exclusively by teaching assistants.

(DfE 2011b: 3.26)

Similarly, in their *Teaching and Learning Toolkit* (2012) which referred to evidence-based research, the Sutton Trust and EEF found that low-attaining pupils did less well with a TA. They commented:

Most studies have consistently found very small or no effect on supported pupils' attainment. There is however some evidence that there is greater impact when teaching assistants are given a particular pedagogical role or responsibility in specific curriculum interventions where the effect appears to be greater, particularly with training and support. Impact in these instances is only half the gains compared with qualified teachers.

(The Sutton Trust–EEF 2012: 28)

Peter Blatchford and colleagues' research report on the deployment and impact of support staff in schools (2009) confirmed the findings of Ofsted, the DfE and the Sutton Trust–EEF: 'Overall, it is worrying that extra support does not have a positive relationship with pupil progress' (Blatchford *et al.* 2009: 132). Blatchford and colleagues gave the following reasons as to why TAs may be having little impact on pupil progress:

- a lack of preparation for support staff and teachers on effective joint working (i.e. having time before and after a lesson to plan and give feedback);
- a lack of sufficient training for teachers on how best to deploy TAs, in relation to pedagogy and the curriculum;
- TAs not knowing how pupils learn, why some pupils fail to learn and which strategies are the most useful to help pupils with SEND to learn;
- a lack of understanding regarding the impact of TA support, whether delivered within or outside the mainstream classroom (e.g. how it can isolate the supported pupil from teacher interaction, reduce the supported pupil's curriculum coverage and challenge, and isolate them from their peers, all of which impact negatively on the supported pupil's progress);
- the informal relationship between the TA and the supported pupil, resulting in more frequent incidental chatter, and less of a focus on pedagogy or talking about learning;
- lower expectations about what pupils with SEND can achieve, due to not understanding smaller-stepped assessment for learning and rates of progress, as well as not knowing what good and adequate progress looks like for a diversity of pupils with SEND.

The effectiveness of TAs

The role of TAs is more effective when they work in partnership with the teacher on joint planning for the inclusion and engagement of pupils with SEND in lessons. In order to maximise the full potential of the TA, teachers need to inform them of the expected learning objectives, outcomes and activities and tasks planned well in advance of the lesson.

The effectiveness of additional TA support is dependent on good two-way open communication existing between the teacher and the TA, who both keep the SENCO informed of the progress of pupils with SEND and of any barriers to learning and participation they may face. Class and subject teachers need to monitor the impact of TA support and interventions, and feed this back to the SENCO.

In their *Special Educational Needs and Disability Review*, Ofsted commented:

> The best learning occurred in all types of provision when teachers or other lead adults had a thorough and detailed knowledge of the children and young people; a thorough knowledge and understanding of teaching and learning strategies and techniques, as well as the subject or areas of learning being taught; and a sound understanding of child development and how different learning difficulties and disabilities influence this.
>
> (Ofsted 2010: 11)

The Sutton Trust–EEF *Teaching and Learning Toolkit* (Higgins *et al.* 2014) once again researched the impact of TAs. Evidence suggested that TAs who provided general class-room support did not make a significant impact on the progress of pupils with SEND. However, where teachers and TAs worked together effectively, there was evidence of an increase in the attainment of pupils with SEND. When TAs provided one-to-one or small-group targeted support, they showed a stronger and more positive benefit, especially when they had been trained and deployed carefully.

There is an excellent archived DCSF resource in relation to the effective deployment of TAs and learning support assistants. This can be accessed at http://webarchive. nationalarchives.gov.uk by searching for the publication entitled *Maximising Progress: Ensuring the Attainment of Pupils with SEN* (2005) and referring to pp. 20–2. There is an excellent monitoring table on p. 21 that could be downloaded and used by class and subject teachers to monitor TAs working in the classroom.

In effectively supported lessons, TAs should:

- be clear about what the pupils with SEND are expected to learn in the lesson;
- build on SEND pupils' prior learning;
- enable pupils with SEND to work independently;
- model good learning approaches to pupils with SEND, during support;
- check and review the SEND pupils' learning at the end of the lesson;
- know what the next steps in their learning will be;
- show evidence of the impact of their support for learning, through improved pupil outcomes.

Class and subject teachers may find Table 6.2 helpful in making judgements about the effective deployment of TAs. It mirrors the type of criteria that Ofsted would make

Table 6.2

Evaluating the deployment of TAs

Grade	Evidence descriptor
Outstanding (1)	– TAs are well directed to support learning. – They make a significant contribution in very effectively supporting SEND pupils' learning and well-being. – They understand the next steps that pupils with SEND need to take, and provide a wide range of learning support activities.
Good (2)	– TAs are well deployed and are effective in what they do. – TAs relate well to the pupils with SEND whom they support and expect them to work hard.
Requires improvement (3)	– TAs are utilised adequately. – They are not effective in supporting learning because they have an incomplete understanding of expectations, and accept SEND pupils' efforts too readily, without a sufficient level of challenge.
Inadequate (4)	– TAs are utilised inadequately due to poor management. – TAs lack the necessary knowledge, skills and understanding, thus contributing little to lessons or to SEND pupils' learning and well-being.

ANNUAL SURVEY OF TEACHING ASSISTANT SUPPORT

Teacher: _____   Teaching Assistant: _____

Pupil: _____   Date: _____

QUESTIONS:

1. When is teaching assistant support most helpful and useful?

2. What is the best type of teaching assistant support from your point of view/for you?

In-class support ☐   Work outside ☐   ICT support/ ☐   Other: (please specify)
                            the classroom   computer
                                                                              _____

                                                                              _____

3. What makes teaching assistant support effective and work well?

4. Do you like being with the same teaching assistant/teacher all year?

   YES ☐   NO ☐

5. What has been the best and greatest teaching assistant achievement this year?

6. When is teaching assistant support least helpful, least effective or most challenging?

7. What would make teaching assistant support even better?

8. Any further comments on teaching assistant support you wish to make:

Thank you for completing this survey. Please return to the SEN Coordinator by the end of the week.

Figure 6.4 Annual survey on the effectiveness of TA support

judgements against. During inspections, Ofsted inspectors will evaluate the use of and contribution made by TAs. Inspectors will have a discussion about teaching and learning with TAs in order to evaluate SEND pupils' learning over time.

Figure 6.4 provides a generic survey that can be completed by class and subject teachers on the effectiveness of TA support.

Effective partnership working with parents and carers of pupils with SEND

Parents and carers are the first prime educators of their children. On average, children spend 87 per cent of their time at home with their parents or carers and other family members. Parents and carers are usually the best judges of what children need. They understand their children better than anyone else; they have important insights into what their child wants. Partnership, in relation to working jointly and productively with parents and carers, refers to a state of 'being' – that the parents and carers of children with SEND are viewed as 'authentic' partners of equal worth, whose contributions are valued and respected by teachers and other professionals, working with and supporting the child or young person.

It is a known fact that children are far more likely to view their education in a positive light and be more receptive to learning when their parents or carers are enthusiastic about and value education.

Any partnership working between teachers and parents or carers of children with SEND must:

- look at helping parents and carers in an enabling way;
- support parents and carers, and not rescue them or do crisis management;
- work 'with' parents and carers rather than 'do things to' them.

The characteristics of effective partnership working with parents and carers

The key characteristics of effective partnership working between teachers and parents and carers of children with SEND include the following:

- the sharing of power, responsibility and ownership for meeting the needs of the child with SEND;
- a degree of mutuality (i.e. listening to each other, engaging in a responsive dialogue with fairness on both sides);
- shared aims and goals based on a common understanding of the needs of the child with SEND;
- a commitment to joint action with parents or carers, educators and other agencies working together to address needs;
- a strong relationship of trust between all parties;
- an equal decision-making relationship between all parties;
- open and honest two-way communication between all parties;
- an appreciation of differences and diversity existing among different families.

The family in the twenty-first century includes the following as parents and carers of children and young people with or without SEND: biological mothers and fathers; adoptive parents; step-parents; same-sex parents; foster carers; legal guardians; grandparents; and extended family members such as aunts, uncles and cousins. The greater diversity in family patterns in the twenty-first century can be attributed to there being more divorce, separation, cohabitation and childbirth outside marriage; marriage and childbearing happening on average later in life; and fertility treatment being made available.

What occurs within the family, whatever its composition, has more impact on a pupil's learning, development and well-being than any other single factor. What families do is far more important than the structure of the family, particularly as they are the first prime educators of their children.

Parents and carers of children with SEND experience additional pressures and anxieties about their child's education and well-being. They may, for example, be sensitive or reactive to a teacher's comments about their child's slower progress. More articulate parents and carers of children with SEND may be over-anxious, readily communicating their concerns about their child's difficulties and lack of progress, while at the same time having high expectations of their child. Alternatively, other parents and carers of children with SEND may lack confidence and rarely attend parents' evenings or review meetings. They may appear to be unconcerned about their child's progress or behaviour. These parents and carers may have had negative schooling experiences themselves, and thus be reluctant to work in partnership with the education setting.

Key principles of working effectively in partnership with parents and carers

Class and subject teachers will need to:

- acknowledge and draw upon parents' and carers' knowledge and experience of their child, as they can offer valuable information in planning support;

- begin a discussion by focusing on the pupil's strengths and achievements;

- recognise the feelings and emotions of parents and carers of pupils with SEND – some may experience feelings of guilt for having a child with SEND;

- go through any documentation or particular SEND procedures with the parents and carers of pupils with SEND, in partnership with the SENCO, to prevent any misunderstandings arising;

- actively listen to what the parents and carers tell them about their child's learning and behaviour at home;

- ensure that they communicate with parents and carers of SEND pupils using their preferred method (e.g. email, telephone, face-to-face meeting, letter, blog);

- keep parents and carers informed about the progress and behaviour of their child in their lessons;

- view parents and carers positively as essential 'partners' in their child's education;

- signpost parents and carers to the 'local offer', as appropriate (e.g. they may welcome their child being able to access a sports club, a play group or a recreational facility in the local community);

- prepare well in advance for EHC plan meetings with parents and carers;

- arrange a future meeting with the parents and carers, if time runs short and there is more to discuss in relation to the pupil's additional provision;
- offer parents and carers practical strategies for supporting their child's learning, behaviour and well-being at home;
- respond promptly to any issues or queries raised by parents and carers;
- ensure that any written reports to parents and carers are clear and concise, and avoid using too much jargon or acronyms.

Using the structured conversation to strengthen communication with parents and carers

The structured conversation with parents and carers of pupils with SEND is a recommended approach in the draft 2014 *SEND Code of Practice*. While it is a very time-consuming process to prepare and operate, it is an extremely empowering approach for parents and carers of pupils with SEND, which can helpfully inform the nature of the additional provision made available to the pupils.

The definition of the structured conversation

The structured conversation as a listening conversation is designed to improve the engagement of parents and carers and to change the nature of the dialogue between parents and carers and the school (i.e. it is open and supportive, and allows for the free exchange of information and views between parents and carers, the school, and the teacher and SENCO). The structured conversation is recommended to form part of the EHC plan review process.

The approach the structured conversation takes focuses on listening to the views of parents and carers, and the pupil with SEND, in order to better understand what they identify as the main barriers to learning and participation. It also enables both parties to identify what they consider has worked well in relation to SEND provision and to say what else they would wish to see in place.

The aims of the structured conversation

Undertaking a structured conversation with parents and carers of pupils with SEND aims to:

- facilitate a more positive relationship that has a shared purpose of improving the educational achievement of the pupil with SEND;
- promote ongoing two-way communication between parents and carers, the child, and the teacher and SENCO, and clarify the most effective means for communication with parents and carers;
- provide a means by which parents and carers can make their contribution heard and understood, and feel reassured that any concerns or views they have expressed will be acted upon;
- build up a greater understanding of the child in their home context;
- draw upon the knowledge parents and carers have of their child (i.e. their child's strengths, what they enjoy and can do well, and the barriers that can get in the way of them making progress and feeling good about themselves);

- help to raise the aspirations of the parents and carers and the school about what the pupil with SEND can attain, through a focus on progress and achieving better outcomes for them;

- develop a genuine trusting collaborative partnership that makes parents and carers feel more confident about engaging with their child's school and teachers, and of taking a greater part in supporting their child's learning and development at home;

- help to clarify the responsibilities of the parents and carers, the pupil with SEND and the school;

- enable parents and carers to participate in identifying the support their child needs in order to meet the agreed set targets and expected outcomes;

- keep parents and carers well informed about their child's progress and next steps in learning;

- use the outcomes from the structured conversation with parents and carers to help to improve the learning, teaching and SEND provision for the pupil with SEND.

Who is involved in the structured conversation

The structured conversation usually takes place between the parent(s) or carer(s) and the class or form teacher, with or without the SENCO. Too many people attending the structured conversation can stifle discussion. Where appropriate, and depending on their age, maturity and understanding, the pupil with SEND should have a chance to join in the structured conversation, at some point.

When the structured conversation should be held

Ideally, the structured conversation should take place each term, to coincide with reviewing the SEND pupil's progress and achievements, as part of the EHC plan review process. It can also be aligned with the education setting's regular cycle of discussions with parents and carers (e.g. parents' evenings or 'meet the teacher' days).

The component parts of the structured conversation

The conversation is structured around four key stages: **Explore**, **Focus**, **Plan** and **Review**. Each stage is intended to open the conversation, in order that general issues can be understood properly, and then discussion narrowed down and focused on key issues and points for subsequent future action, target setting, and the review and summing-up of what has been discussed and agreed at the meeting. Each stage of the structured conversation is explained in more depth in Table 6.3, which acts as a useful aide memoire to the process for class or form teachers leading the discussion.

The class or form teacher leading the structured conversation will need to make notes recording the key points arising from discussion with parents or carers. Figure 6.5 provides a model template for recording these key points.

The teacher leading the structured conversation with parents or carers of EHC plan pupils should remember that there needs to be a balance between celebratory positive comments and constructive critical feedback during discussion.

The first initial structured conversation in the term should agree upon:

- the aims of the conversation;

- the time available for the conversation;

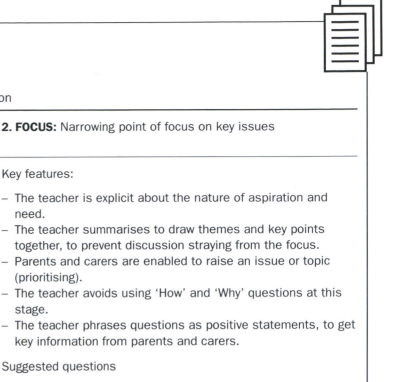

Table 6.3

The component parts of the structured conversation

---

1. EXPLORE: Opening up to explore and understand

Key features:

- The non-verbal cues of the teacher put parents and carers at ease.
- The teacher is attentive and listens actively.
- Silence is used to allow parents and carers thinking time.
- The teacher paraphrases what parents or carers have said to check understanding.
- The teacher shows empathy.
- The teacher asks questions to elicit parents' or carers' hopes and aspirations for their child.

Suggested questions:

- What do you consider are the needs of your child?
- What do you want for your child in school?
- What have been the barriers to your child achieving?
- What has worked well in the past to help your child learn?
- What do you feel are the limits to your child's potential?

2. FOCUS: Narrowing point of focus on key issues

Key features:

- The teacher is explicit about the nature of aspiration and need.
- The teacher summarises to draw themes and key points together, to prevent discussion straying from the focus.
- Parents and carers are enabled to raise an issue or topic (prioritising).
- The teacher avoids using 'How' and 'Why' questions at this stage.
- The teacher phrases questions as positive statements, to get key information from parents and carers.

Suggested questions

- Can you tell me something more about when your child . . .?
- What could you do differently at home with your child next time . . .?
- Have you any idea why the approach you suggest might work better?

---

3. PLAN: Actions to address key issues and priorities

Key features:

- The teacher gives parents and carers information on their child's provision, progress and achievements to enable them to make a decision as to whether the SEND provision is OK or needs changing.
- Agreed targets that have a level of challenge are set.
- Parents and carers are consulted on how they feel they can help their child at home.
- The teacher clarifies what strategies and interventions are being put in place at school.
- Parents and carers are consulted on timescales and success criteria to evaluate the impact of provision.
- The teacher clarifies the ongoing assessment of the child's progress.
- A plan is produced as an outcome of the conversation, which is clear and concise and includes long-term and short-term goals.

4. REVIEW: Summary of key points and clarify next steps

Key features:

- The teacher summarises the main points:

  - We have talked about . . . today.
  - We have identified the areas we agree are important to target for improvement.
  - This is the agreed plan to put in place.
  - Do you feel the plan will work?
  - Can you see a difference in your child?

- The teacher agrees on how parent and carers wish to communicate for the follow-up.
- Dates for next meetings are agreed.
- A named contact in school is provided.
- The teacher seeks feedback from parents and carers on how they felt the discussion went.

Suggested questions:

- How well do you feel today's meeting has gone?
- Is there anything else you want to tell me or add?
- Have we missed anything important?
- Do you feel we have listened well enough, understood and appreciated the issues you raised?
- Is there anything else you want to ask about the next steps or the outcomes from today's meeting?

Structured conversation stage	Parents'/carers' views, concerns, issues and comments Key points	Teacher's/SENCO's comments Key points
Explore		
Focus		
Plan		
Review		

Figure 6.5 Template for recording key points arising from a structured conversation

- the protocols for confidentiality;
- the number of structured conversations (review meetings) required in the academic year.

Subsequent structured conversations, following the initial discussion, should focus on the progress the pupil with SEND has made against the agreed targets, and if the SEND provision and plan of action needs amending.

The best source of reference for the structured conversation can be found in an archived DCSF publication entitled *Achievement for All: The Structured Conversation – Handbook to Support Training* (2009).

Questions for reflection

1 Teamwork is an aspect of your wider role that you wish to develop further. How will you make best use of a coaching or mentoring partnership, to help you to address this issue?

2 You are new to working in partnership with an outreach teacher from the local autism team. How will you go about ensuring that you both work effectively together in the classroom, in order to meet the needs of a pupil with ASD?

3 The SENCO has set aside some quality time for you to meet with them to discuss your role in undertaking a pupil's EHC plan review. Make a list of possible questions you would wish to ask the SENCO that would enable you to feel more confident about leading this first EHC plan review.

4 A new TA has been assigned to one of your classes, and they appear to be unclear about how to evaluate the impact of their support for learning. How will you go about working in partnership with them to address this issue?

5 You have been asked to join a school working party that is looking at how to improve partnership working with the parents and carers of pupils with SEND. What valuable contributions do you feel you can make to the work of this team?

Glossary

Accountability is the acknowledgement and assumption of responsibility for actions, decisions and policies, and for reporting, explaining and being answerable for resulting consequences.

Achievement for All is a school improvement programme that has a particular focus on raising the aspirations, access and achievements of the lowest 20 per cent of learners in schools, which includes pupils with SEND.

Assessment uses a range of measures to collect the necessary information about a child or young person's attainment, progress and well-being in order to inform the next steps in meeting their needs.

Assessment for learning (AfL) is the process of seeking and interpreting evidence for use by pupils and their teachers to decide where pupils are in their learning, where they need to go next and how to get there.

Bullying is any behaviour by an individual or group that is repeated over time and that intentionally hurts another individual or group, either physically or emotionally. It is often motivated by prejudice against a particular group, based on race, gender, religion, disability or sexual orientation.

Coaching is a structured sustained process that enables the development of a specific aspect of a professional learner's practice and that is solution-focused in its approach.

Cyber-bullying is the act of using internet or digital (mobile) technologies to upset or humiliate another individual.

Developmental milestones mark the achievement of certain abilities and signal the end of one developmental period and the beginning of another.

Differentiation refers to the process by which curriculum objectives, teaching methods, assessment, resources and learning activities are planned and adjusted to cater for, and match the needs of, pupils with SEND.

Disability describes a physical or mental impairment that has a substantial and long-term effect on an individual's ability to carry out daily activities.

An **Education, Health and Care (EHC) plan** is an outcome-focused plan that favours a person-centred approach to planning and reviewing multi-agency additional provision for children and young people with more complex and severe SEND, aged between 0 and 25, who would have previously have had a statement of SEND or an LDA. The plan also specifies how the personal budget for SEND is to be used.

Emotional intelligence is the ability to recognise, understand, manage and appropriately express emotions. It is about managing yourself and your emotions, and understanding and interpreting the emotions and feelings of others.

Formative assessment is the ongoing assessment undertaken at regular intervals of a pupil's progress, with accompanying feedback to help them to improve further.

The **graduated approach** offers class and subject teachers a four-part cycle to providing SEN Support for those pupils identified with SEND who do not require or already have an EHC plan. Its cycle comprises four stages of action: assess, plan, do and review.

High-incidence SEND are those that can be catered for most frequently in mainstream education settings. They may include SpLD such as dyslexia; SLCN; and sensory impairments.

High-quality teaching is that which is differentiated and personalised to meet the needs of the majority of pupils, including those with SEND. Previously referred to as 'quality first teaching', it is part of the daily repertoire of teaching strategies that ensures SEND pupils' progression in learning.

Long-term memory refers to the permanent storage of knowledge in memory stores located in various parts of the brain. Retrieval from long-term memory is aided by meaning. Unless meaning is attached to new learning, retrieval will be difficult.

Mentoring refers to the help given by a more experienced professional to another colleague who is less experienced to enable them make significant transitions in knowledge, work or thinking.

Meta-cognition refers to 'learning to learn', 'knowing about knowing' and 'thinking about thinking'. It refers to a pupil's awareness of their own knowledge; what they do and do not know; and their ability to understand, control and manipulate their own cognitive processes. It includes when and where to use particular meta-cognitive skills and strategies to promote learning and solve problems.

Outcomes refers to identifiable (positive or negative) impacts of interventions, strategies, programmes, activities and high-quality teaching on children and young people.

P levels are smaller-stepped differentiated performance criteria used for assessing the progress of pupils with SEND aged between five and sixteen, who are working below national curriculum level 1.

Partnership is a collaborative professional relationship designed to produce positive educational and social effects on a child or young person while also being mutually beneficial to all other parties involved. Professional partnerships are characterised by common aims, mutual respect, negotiation and flexibility.

The **person-centred approach** refers to the process of continual listening and learning, focusing on what is important to the child or young person now and in the future, and acting upon this information, in alliance with their family and friends. It is an approach which is recommended to support the EHC plan process.

Progress of pupils with SEND is judged in relation to their age and prior attainment (starting point) either over a period of time, such as an academic year, or at the end of a Key Stage.

The **pupil premium** is additional funding targeted at young children and pupils who are on FSM, who are LAC or who are from an armed service family. The money is used by early years settings and schools to help to close the attainment gap between these vulnerable disadvantaged children and young people and their more socially and economically advantaged peers.

RAISEonline is a web-based system that contains data about a school's basic characteristics, attainment and progress in the core subjects, to support evaluation and target setting.

Reading age is where a pupil's ability to read at a given age is tested and compared with the average reading ability of other children of that same age. The comparison produces a reading age.

Reasonable adjustments refers to removing barriers to participation and learning for children and young people with disabilities, to prevent them being at a substantial disadvantage compared to other peers without a disability. It relates to ensuring access to the curriculum, to information in different formats and to buildings.

Self-esteem is the way individuals see, think and feel about themselves. It also relates to how individuals judge their self-worth, as well as how they think others perceive and feel about them.

Self-regulation refers to pupils managing their own motivation towards learning and maintaining motivation in order to complete a given task, which is a meta-cognitive skill. Self-regulation also refers to the cognitive aspects of thinking and reasoning (i.e. being able to use the right approaches and to modify learning strategies and skills based on their awareness of effectiveness).

SEN Support is a school-based single category that adopts a graduated approach to meeting the needs of those children and young people identified with SEND without an EHC plan, who would have previously been those on Action and Action Plus.

Short-term memory refers to the storage of information for a matter of seconds, without having to manipulate it in any way.

Special educational needs (SEN) refers to a child or young person having a learning difficulty that calls for special educational provision to be made for them. A learning difficulty means that they have significantly greater difficulty in learning than most children of the same age.

A **special educational needs coordinator (SENCO)** is responsible for the day-to-day operation of a school's/setting's SEND policy and for coordinating the additional support for pupils with SEND. They have to be a qualified teacher.

Special educational provision is educational or training provision that is additional or different from that made generally for other children and young people of the same age.

A **specialist leader of education (SLE)** is an outstanding middle or senior leader, who supports their colleagues in similar positions in other schools to improve a whole-school aspect, such as SEND provision, behaviour, a curriculum subject or a phase of education, such as early years.

Structured conversation supports the greater engagement of parents and carers of children and young people with SEND by enabling them to make their contributions heard and understood by teachers, the SENCO and the wider school.

Summative assessment is the summary of a pupil's overall learning or final achievement at the end of an academic year or a course of study.

Teaching schools are outstanding schools that identify and share good practice existing in their own organisations with their alliance partner schools, and among other schools that are in need of improvement. Teaching schools also provide training and professional development opportunities for trainee, newly qualified and experienced teachers.

Value added is a measure that shows the difference a school makes to the educational outcomes of pupils given their starting points.

Vulnerable children refers to those pupils who are at risk of social exclusion, those who are disadvantaged and those whose life chances are likely to be jeopardised unless more action is taken to meet their needs.

Well-being refers to having the basic things required to live and be healthy, safe and happy.

Working memory refers to the retention of information in short-term (temporary) storage while processing incoming information and retrieving information from long-term storage.

References and further reading

(All websites accessed on 4 September 2014.)

ABA/CaF (2011) *Bullying of Children with Disabilities and Special Educational Needs in Schools: Briefing Paper for Parents on the Views and Experiences of Other Parents, Carers and Families.* London: Anti-Bullying Alliance. Available at www.anti-bullyingalliance.org.uk/media/2254/SEND_bullying_briefing_Contact-a-Family-and-ABA_parents.pdf

ABA/CaF (2012) *Cyberbullying and Children and Young People with SEN and Disabilities: Guidance for Teachers and Other Professionals.* London: Anti-Bullying Alliance. Available at www.anti-bullyingalliance.org.uk/media/7441/cyberbullying-and-send-module-final.pdf

Allison, S. & Harbour, M. (2009) *The Coaching Toolkit: A Practical Guide for Your School.* London: SAGE

Autism Education Trust (2012) *Do You Have a Child with Autism in Your Class? A Guide for Teachers.* Available at www.autismeducationtrust.org.uk/resources/teachers%20guide.aspx

Blatchford, P., Bassett, P., Brown, P., Koutsoubou, M., Martin, P., Russell, A. & Webster, R. with Rubie-Davies, C. (2009) *Deployment and Impact of Support Staff in Schools: The Impact of Support Staff in Schools – Results from Strand 2 Wave 2.* DCSF-RR148. London: Institute of Education, University of London. Available at www.ioe.ac.uk/documents/DISS_Strand_2_Wave_2_Report.pdf

Burnett, G. (2003) *Learning to Learn: Introductory Workbook.* Carmarthen: Crown House Publishing Ltd

Cheminais, R. (2008) *Every Child Matters: A Practical Guide for Teaching Assistants.* London: Routledge

Cheminais, R. (2009) *Effective Multi-Agency Partnerships: Putting Every Child Matters into Practice.* London: SAGE

Cheminais, R. (2010) *Special Educational Needs for Newly Qualified Teachers and Teaching Assistants: A Practical Guide.* London: Routledge

Cheminais, R. (2013) *Promoting and Delivering School-to-School Support for Special Educational Needs: A Practical Guide for SENCOs.* London: Routledge

The Communication Trust (2011) *Misunderstood: Supporting Children and Young People with Speech, Language and Communication Needs.* London: The Communication Trust/Early Support. Available at www.thecommunicationtrust.org.uk/media/3670/misunderstood_edition_2_final.pdf

CUREE (2005) *Mentoring and Coaching CPD Capacity Building Project: National Framework for Mentoring and Coaching.* Coventry: Centre for the Use of Research & Evidence in Education. Available at www.curee.co.uk/files/publication/1301587364/MC%20Framework%2010.pdf

DCSF (2005) *Maximising Progress: Ensuring the Attainment of Pupils with SEN.* Annesley: Department for Children, Schools and Families. Available at http://webarchive.nationalarchives.gov.uk/20110202093118/http:/nationalstrategies.standards.dcsf.gov.uk/node/97233

DCSF (2006) *Effective Leadership: Ensuring the Progress of Pupils with SEN and/or Disabilities.* Annesley: Department for Children, Schools and Families. Available at www.learntogether.org.uk/resources/Documents/SNS%20Effective%20Leadership.pdf

DCSF (2009) *Achievement for All: The Structured Conversation – Handbook to Support Training.* Annesley: Department for Children, Schools and Families. Available at www.aettraininghubs.org.uk/wp-content/uploads/2012/05/23.3-Structured-Conversation-Handbook.pdf

DfE (2010a) *The Importance of Teaching: The Schools White Paper 2010.* Norwich: The Stationery Office. Available at www.gov.uk/government/uploads/system/uploads/attachment_data/file/175429/CM-7980.pdf

DfE (2010b) *Progression 2010–11: Advice on Improving Data to Raise Attainment and Maximise the Progress of Learners with Special Educational Needs.* London: Department for Education. Available at www.gov.uk/government/uploads/system/uploads/attachment_data/file/180840/DfE-00557-2010.pdf

DfE (2011a) *Getting the Simple Things Right: Charlie Taylor's Behaviour Checklists*. London: Department for Education. Available at www.gov.uk/government/uploads/system/uploads/attachment_data/file/283997/charlie_taylor_checklist.pdf

DfE (2011b) *Support and Aspiration: A New Approach to Special Educational Needs and Disability – A Consultation*. Norwich: The Stationery Office. Available at http://webarchive.nationalarchives.gov.uk/20130401151715/https://www.education.gov.uk/publications/eorderingdownload/green-paper-sen.pdf

DfE (2012a) *NFER Teacher Voice Omnibus February 2012 Survey: Pupil Behaviour*. London: Department for Education. Available at www.gov.uk/government/uploads/system/uploads/attachment_data/file/205871/DFE-RR219.pdf

DfE (2012b) *Support and Aspiration: A New Approach to Special Educational Needs and Disability – Progress and Next Steps*. London: Department for Education. Available at www.gov.uk/government/uploads/system/uploads/attachment_data/file/180836/DFE-00046-2012.pdf

DfE (2012c) *Draft Legislation on Reform of Provision for Children and Young People with Special Educational Needs*. London: The Stationery Office. Available at www.educationengland.org.uk/documents/pdfs/2012-white-sen-reform.pdf

DfE (2013a) *The Young Person's Guide to the Children and Families Bill*. London: Department for Education. Available at www.gov.uk/government/uploads/system/uploads/attachment_data/file/189968/Young_person_s_guide_to_the_Children_and_Families_Bill.pdf

DfE (2013b) *Equality Act 2010: Advice for Schools*. London: Department for Education. Available at www.gov.uk/government/uploads/system/uploads/attachment_data/file/315587/Equality_Act_Advice_Final.pdf

DfE (2013c) *Reforming the Accountability System for Secondary Schools: Government Response to the February to May 2013 Consultation on Secondary School Accountability*. London: Department for Education. Available at www.gov.uk/government/uploads/system/uploads/attachment_data/file/249893/Consultation_response_Secondary_School_Accountability_Consultation_14-Oct-13_v3.pdf

DfE (2013d) *Indicative Draft: The (0 to 25) Special Educational Needs Code of Practice*. London: Department for Education. Available at www.devon.gov.uk/text/sc-mar136002.pdf

DfE (2013e) *Preventing and Tackling Bullying: Advice for Headteachers, Staff and Governing Bodies*. London: Department for Education. Available at www.gov.uk/government/uploads/system/uploads/attachment_data/file/288444/preventing_and_tackling_bullying_march14.pdf

DfE (2013f) *Teachers' Standards: Guidance for School Leaders, School Staff and Governing Bodies*. London: Department for Education. Available at www.gov.uk/government/uploads/system/uploads/attachment_data/file/301107/Teachers__Standards.pdf

DfE (2013g) *NFER Teacher Voice Omnibus May 2013 Survey: Pupil Behaviour*. London: Department for Education. Available at www.gov.uk/government/uploads/system/uploads/attachment_data/file/210297/DFE-RR304.pdf

DfE (2013h) *The National Curriculum in England: Framework Document*. London: Department for Education. Available at www.gov.uk/government/uploads/system/uploads/attachment_data/file/210969/NC_framework_document_-_FINAL.pdf

DfE/DH (2013i) *Draft Special Educational Needs (SEN) Code of Practice: For 0 to 25 Years – Statutory Guidance for Organisations Who Work with and Support Children and Young People with SEN*. London: Department for Education and the Department of Health. Available at www.education.gov.uk/consultations/downloadableDocs/Draft%20SEN%20Code%20of%20Practice.pdf

DfE (2013j) *Working Together to Safeguard Children: A Guide to Inter-Agency Working to Safeguard and Promote the Welfare of Children*. London: Department for Education. Available at www.gov.uk/government/uploads/system/uploads/attachment_data/file/281368/Working_together_to_safeguard_children.pdf

DfE/DH (2014a) *Governors' Handbook: For Governors in Maintained Schools, Academies and Free Schools*. London: Department for Education and Department of Health. Available at www.gov.uk/government/uploads/system/uploads/attachment_data/file/270398/Governors-Handbook-January-2014.pdf

DfE (2014b) *Behaviour and Discipline in Schools: Advice for Headteachers and School Staff*. London: Department for Education. Available from www.gov.uk/government/uploads/system/uploads/attachment_data/file/277894/Behaviour_and_Discipline_in_Schools_-a_guide_for_headteachers_and_school_staff.pdf

DfE (2014c) *Reforming Assessment and Accountability for Primary Schools: Government Response to Consultation on Primary School Assessment and Accountability*. London: Department for Education. Available at www.gov.uk/government/uploads/system/uploads/attachment_data/file/297595/Primary_Accountability_and_Assessment_Consultation_Response.pdf

DfE (2014d) *Special Educational Needs and Disability: Research Priorities and Questions*. London: Department for Education. Available at www.gov.uk/government/uploads/system/uploads/attachment_data/file/288089/SEN_Research_Priorities_and_Questions_Final_Draft.pdf

DfE (2014e) *The SEN and Disability Pathfinder Programme Evaluation: Progress and Indicative Costs of the Reforms – Research Report*. London: Department for Education. Available at www.gov.uk/government/uploads/system/uploads/attachment_data/file/298842/SEND_Pathfinder_Evaluation_Progress_Research_Report_Dec_2013.pdf

References and further reading

DfE/DH (2014f) *Implementing a New 0 to 25 Special Needs System: LAs and Partners – Further Government Advice for Local Authorities and Health Partners*. London: Department for Education and Department of Health. Available at http://socialwelfare.bl.uk/subject-areas/services-client-groups/children-disabilities/departmentforeducation/162792Implementing_a_new_0_to_25_special_needs_system_LAs_and_partners_-_April_2014.pdf

DfE (2014g) *Draft Special Educational Needs and Disability Code of Practice: 0 to 25 Years – Statutory Guidance for Organisations Who Work with and Support Children and Young People with Special Educational Needs and Disabilities*. London: Department for Education and Department of Health. Available at www.gov.uk/government/uploads/system/uploads/attachment_data/file/342440/SEND_Code_of_Practice_approved_by_Parliament_29.07.14.pdf

DfE (2014h) *Keeping Children Safe in Education: Statutory Guidance for Schools and Colleges*. London: Department for Education. Available at www.gov.uk/government/uploads/system/uploads/attachment_data/file/350747/Keeping_children_safe_in_education.pdf

DfE (2014i) *Keeping Children Safe in Education: Information for All School and College Staff*. London: Department for Education. Available at www.gov.uk/government/uploads/system/uploads/attachment_data/file/300319/KCSIE_FINAL_8PG.pdf

DfE (2014j) *National Curriculum and Assessment from September 2014: Information for Schools*. London: Department for Education. Available at www.gov.uk/government/uploads/system/uploads/attachment_data/file/347985/National_curriculum_and_assessment_from_September_2014.pdf

DfE (2014k) *Consultation on Draft Guidance for Supporting Pupils at School with Medical Conditions: Summary of Responses*. London: Department for Education. Available at www.gov.uk/government/uploads/system/uploads/attachment_data/file/307228/medical_conditions_consultation_report_-_publication_version.pdf

DfE (2014l) *Statistical First Release: Level 2 and 3 Attainment by Young People in England Measured Using Matched Administrative Data – Attainment by Age 19 in 2013*. London: Department for Education. Available at www.gov.uk/government/uploads/system/uploads/attachment_data/file/295696/SFR_10-2014.pdf

DfE (2014m) *Update on Progress 8 Measure and Reforms to Secondary School Accountability Framework*. London: Department for Education. Available at www.gov.uk/government/uploads/system/uploads/attachment_data/file/269438/update_progress_8_measure_secondary_school_accountability_framework_reforms.pdf

DfE (2014n) *Progress 8 Measure in 2016: Technical Guide for Maintained Secondary Schools, Academies and Free Schools*. London: Department for Education. Available at www.gov.uk/government/uploads/system/uploads/attachment_data/file/314294/Progress_8_measure_in_2016.pdf

DfE (2014o) *Supporting Pupils at School with Medical Conditions: Statutory Guidance for Governing Bodies of Maintained Schools and Proprietors of Academies in England. Draft*. London: Department for Education. Available at www.gov.uk/government/uploads/system/uploads/attachment_data/file/277025/draft_statutory_guidance_on_supporting_pupils_at_school_with_medical_conditions_for_consultation.pdf

DfES (2005) *Promoting Inclusion and Tackling Underperformance: Maximising Progress: Ensuring the Attainment of Pupils with SEN. Part 2: Approaches to Learning and Teaching in the Mainstream Classroom*. Norwich: Department for Education and Skills. Available at www.suffolkmaths.co.uk/pages/SEN/SENCO%20Training/Part%202-SEN-0105-2005G.pdf

DfES (2006) *Promoting Inclusion and Tackling Underperformance: Effective Leadership: Ensuring the Progress of Pupils with SEN and/or Disabilities*. Norwich: Department for Education and Skills. Available at www.learntogether.org.uk/resources/Documents/SNS%20Effective%20Leadership.pdf

Dryden, G. & Vos, J. (2001) *The Learning Revolution: To Change the Way the World Learns*. Stafford: Network Educational Press Ltd

East, V. & Evans, L. (2006) *At a Glance: A Practical Guide to Children's Special Needs*. Second edition. London: Continuum International Publishing Group

EHRC (2010a) *New Equality Act Guidance*. Available at www.equalityhumanrights.com/advice-and-guidance/new-equality-act-guidance/

EHRC (2010b) *Equality Act 2010: Education Providers – Schools' Guidance*. Available at www.equalityhumanrights.com/advice-and-guidance/new-equality-act-guidance/

Ginnis, P. (2004) *The Teacher's Toolkit: Raise Classroom Achievement with Strategies for Every Learner*. Carmarthen: Crown House Publishing Ltd

Higgins, S., Katsipataki, M., Kokotsaki, D., Coleman, R., Major, L.E. & Coe, R. (2014) *The Sutton Trust–Education Endowment Foundation Teaching and Learning Toolkit*. London: Education Endowment Trust

Home Learning College (2007) *Section 1 Child and Young Person Development*. London: Home Learning College. Available at www.homelearningcollege.com

Long, R. (2000a) *Classroom Survival Skills*. Totnes: Rob Long's Education Works

Long, R. (2000b) *Supporting Troubled Children*. Totnes: Rob Long's Education Works

Long, R. (2000c) *Making Sense of Teenagers*. Totnes: Rob Long's Education Works

McAfee (2014) *Digital Deception: The Online Behaviour of Teens*. Santa Clara, CA. Available at www.anti-bullyingalliance.org.uk/media/6621/mcafee_digital-deception_the-online-behaviour-of-teens.pdf

Matthews, P. & Berwick, G. (2013) *Teaching Schools: First among Equals?* Nottingham: National College for Teaching and Leadership. Available at http://schoolpartnerships.co.uk/wp-content/uploads/teaching-schools-first-among-equals-NCSL-2013.pdf

Meyer, B., Haywood, N., Sachdev, D., & Faraday, S. (2008) *Independent Learning: Literature Review.* Research Report No. DCSF-RR051. Annesley: Department for Children, School and Families. Available at www.gov.uk/government/uploads/system/uploads/attachment_data/file/222277/DCSF-RR051.pdf

NAHT (2014) *Report of the NAHT Commission on Assessment.* Haywards Heath: National Association of Head Teachers. Available at www.naht.org.uk/welcome/news-and-media/key-topics/assessment/assessment-commission-resources/

nasen (2013) *The nasen Guide to SEN.* Tamworth: National Association for Special Educational Needs

nasen (2014a) *A Whole School Approach to Improving Access, Participation and Achievement: Primary Phase.* Tamworth: National Association for Special Needs. Available at www.nasentraining.org.uk/primary-training

nasen (2014b) *A Whole School Approach to Improving Access, Participation and Achievement: Secondary Phase.* Tamworth: National Association for Special Needs. Available at www.nasentraining.org.uk/training-pack

NCSL (2012) *How Teaching Schools Are Already Starting to Make a Difference.* Nottingham: National College for School Leadership. Available at www.gov.uk/government/uploads/system/uploads/attachment_data/file/330522/how-teaching-schools-are-making-a-difference-part-1.pdf

NCSL (2013) *How Teaching Schools Are Making a Difference: Part 2.* Nottingham: National College for School Leadership. Available at www.gov.uk/government/uploads/system/uploads/attachment_data/file/330579/how-teaching-schools-are-making-a-difference-part-2.pdf

NGA (2013a) *Knowing Your School: The FFT Governor Dashboard for Primary School Governors.* London: National Governors' Association. Available at www.nga.org.uk/getattachment/Can-we-help/Knowing-Your-School/Knowing_your_school_5b_NGA_FFT_Primary_FINAL-%282%29.pdf.aspx

NGA (2013b) *Knowing Your School: The FFT Governor Dashboard for Secondary School Governors.* London: National Governors' Association. Available at www.fft.org.uk/FFT/media/fft/Downloads/Knowing_your_school_FFT_Secondary.pdf

NGA (2014a) *Knowing Your School: RAISEonline for Governors of Primary Schools.* Second edition. London: National Governors' Association. Available at www.nga.org.uk/getattachment/Can-we-help/Knowing-Your-School/Knowing-Your-School/Knowing-Your-School-Primary-RAISE-%28Jan-14%29-FINAL.pdf.aspx

NGA (2014b) *Knowing Your School: RAISEonoline for Governors of Secondary Schools.* Second edition. London: National Governors' Association. Available at www.nga.org.uk/getattachment/Can-we-help/Knowing-Your-School/Knowing-Your-School-Secondary-RAISE-%28Jan-14%29-FINAL.pdf.aspx

Ofqual (2014) *Consultation on Setting the Grade Standards of New GCSEs in England.* Coventry: Office of Qualifications and Examinations Regulation. Available at www.ofqual.gov.uk

Ofsted (2010) *Special Educational Needs and Disability Review: A Statement Is Not Enough.* Manchester: Office for Standards in Education, Children's Services and Skills. Available at http://dera.ioe.ac.uk/1145/1/Special%20education%20needs%20and%20disability%20review.pdf

Ofsted (2013a) *The Pupil Premium: How Schools Are Spending the Funding Successfully to Maximise Achievement.* Manchester: Office for Standards in Education, Children's Services and Skills. Available at www.ofsted.gov.uk/sites/default/files/documents/surveys-and-good-practice/t/The%20Pupil%20Premium%20-%20How%20schools%20are%20spending%20the%20funding.pdf

Ofsted (2013b) *The Pupil Premium: Analysis and Challenge Tools for Schools.* Manchester: Office for Standards in Education, Children's Services and Skills. Available at www.ofsted.gov.uk/sites/default/files/documents/surveys-and-good-practice/t/The%20Pupil%20Premium%20-%20Analysis%20and%20challenge%20tools%20for%20schools.pdf

Ofsted (2014a) *School Inspection Handbook: Handbook for Inspecting Schools in England under Section 5 of the Education Act 2005.* Reference No. 120101. Manchester: Office for Standards in Education, Children's Services and Skills. Available at www.ofsted.gov.uk/sites/default/files/documents/inspection--forms-and-guides/s/School%20inspection%20handbook.pdf

Ofsted (2014b) *The Framework for School Inspection: The Framework for Inspecting Schools in England under Section 5 of the Education Act 2005 (as amended).* Reference No. 120100. Manchester: Office for Standards in Education, Children's Services and Skills. Available at www.ofsted.gov.uk/sites/default/files/documents/inspection--forms-and-guides/t/The%20framework%20for%20school%20inspection.pdf

Ofsted (2014c) *Subsidiary Guidance: Supporting the Inspection of Maintained Schools and Academies.* Reference No. 110166. Manchester: Office for Standards in Education, Children's Services and Skills. Available at www.ofsted.gov.uk

Ofsted (2014d) *Inspecting Equalities: Briefing for Section 5 Inspection.* Manchester: Office for Standards in Education, Children's Services and Skills. Available at http://dera.ioe.ac.uk/18231/1/Inspecting%20equalities%20briefing.docx

Reid, G. (2007) *Motivating Learners in the Classroom: Ideas and Strategies.* London: Paul Chapman Publishing

Sanderson, H. (2013) *Using Person-Centred Practices in Schools*. Stockport: HSA Press

Smith, J. (2007) 'Questioning', in *Gifted and Talented UPDATE*, 47: 10. London: Optimus Education

The Sutton Trust–EEF (2012) *Teaching and Learning Toolkit*. London: The Sutton Trust–Education Endowment Foundation. Available at www.educationendowmentfoundation.org.uk/toolkit/.

Websites

www.advanced-training.org.uk/

www.antibullyingalliance.org.uk

www.ask-nanny.com/child-development.htm

www.beatbullying.org

www.childline.org.uk

www.childnet.com/resources

www.complexneeds.org.uk

www.councilfordisabledchildren.org

www.education.gov.uk

www.familylives.org.uk

www.fischertrust.org

www.gov.uk/government/publications

http://gunning-fog-index.com

www.idponline.org.uk

www.kidscape.org.uk/cyberbullying

www.nga.org.uk

www.ofqual.gov.uk

www.ofsted.gov.uk

www.psychology.about.com

www.raiseonline.org

www.roblong.co.uk

www.thinkuknow.co.uk

Index

Page numbers followed by 'f' refer to figures and followed by 't' refer to tables.